A HANDBOOK FOR
Developing & Using Proficiency Scales
IN THE CLASSROOM

Jan K. Hoegh

WITH

Tammy Heflebower
Philip B. Warrick

FOREWORD BY
ROBERT J. MARZANO

555 North Morton Street
Bloomington, IN 47404
888.849.0851
FAX: 866.801.1447

email: info@MarzanoResources.com
MarzanoResources.com

Visit **MarzanoResources.com/reproducibles** to download the free reproducibles in this book.

Printed in the United States of America

Library of Congress Control Number: 2019902672

ISBN: 978-1-943360-27-7

Production Team

President and Publisher: Douglas M. Rife
Associate Publisher: Sarah Payne-Mills
Art Director: Rian Anderson
Managing Production Editor: Kendra Slayton
Production Editor: Laurel Hecker
Content Development Specialist: Amy Rubenstein
Proofreader: Elisabeth Abrams
Text and Cover Designer: Abigail Bowen
Editorial Assistant: Sarah Ludwig

Acknowledgments

This book is dedicated to my three beloved daughters, Leslie, Abby, and Ashlyn, who motivate me daily to set an example worth following and to model what I truly believe—that there are no limits for those who work diligently to pursue their dreams and follow their hearts.

I'd also like to express gratitude to my friend, colleague, and mentor, Dr. Robert Marzano. This book was made possible because of the God-given opportunity to learn from and work alongside him.

Lastly, a huge thank you to the teachers, schools, and districts who willingly shared their examples, stories, and other contributions to this book. I am fortunate to know you and to have been in your learning environments. Keep doing amazing work as educators!

Marzano Resources would like to thank the following reviewers:

Bonnie Nieves
Science Teacher
Millbury Memorial Junior/
   Senior High School
Millbury, Massachusetts

Alex Olson
Principal
Fairview Park Elementary
Spencer, Iowa

Geri Parscale
Solution Tree Associate
Lawrence, Kansas

Heidi Paterson
Science Teacher
Preeceville School
Preeceville, Saskatchewan,
   Canada

Christina Podraza
Assistant Principal
Hawthorne Elementary School
Elmhurst, Illinois

Tara Reed
Fourth-Grade Teacher
Hawk Elementary School
Corinth, Texas

Visit **MarzanoResources.com/reproducibles** to download the reproducibles in this book.

Table of Contents

Reproducible pages are in italics.

About the Authors

Jan K. Hoegh has been an educator for over thirty years and an author and associate for Marzano Resources since 2010. Prior to joining the Marzano team, she was a classroom teacher, building leader, professional development specialist, high school assistant principal, curriculum coordinator, and assistant director of statewide assessment for the Nebraska Department of Education, where her primary focus was Nebraska State Accountability test development. Ms. Hoegh has served on a variety of statewide and national standards and assessment committees and has presented at numerous conferences around the world.

As an associate with Marzano Resources, Jan works with educators across the United States and beyond as they strive to improve student achievement. Her passion for education, combined with extensive knowledge of curriculum, instruction, and assessment, provides credible support for teachers, leaders, schools, and districts. A primary training focus for Ms. Hoegh is high-quality classroom assessment and grading practices. She is coauthor of *Collaborative Teams That Transform Schools* and *A School Leader's Guide to Standards-Based Grading*, as well as other publications.

Jan holds a bachelor of arts in elementary education and a master of arts in educational administration, both from the University of Nebraska at Kearney. She also earned a specialization in assessment from the University of Nebraska–Lincoln.

Tammy Heflebower, EdD, is a highly sought-after school leader and consultant with vast experiences in urban, rural, and suburban districts throughout the United States, Australia, Canada, Denmark, Great Britain, and the Netherlands. Dr. Heflebower has served as an award-winning classroom teacher, building leader, district leader, regional professional development director, and national and international trainer. She has also been an adjunct professor of curriculum, instruction, and assessment at several universities, and a prominent member and leader of numerous statewide and national educational organizations. Dr. Heflebower was vice president and then senior scholar at Marzano Resources and continues to work as an author and associate with Marzano Resources and Solution Tree. In addition, she is the CEO of her own company, !nspire Inc.: Education and Business Solutions, specializing in powerful presentation and facilitation techniques and writing about and sharing them worldwide.

Dr. Heflebower is sole author of the *Presenting Perfected* book series. She is lead author of the award-winning *A School Leader's Guide to Standards-Based Grading*, lead author of the award-finalist *A Teacher's Guide to Standards-Based Learning*, coauthor of *Collaborative Teams That Transform Schools: The Next Step in PLCs* and *Teaching and Assessing 21st Century Skills*, as well as contributing author to over a dozen other books and publications, many of which have been translated into multiple languages and referenced internationally.

Dr. Heflebower holds a bachelor of arts from Hastings College where she was honored as Outstanding Young Alumna and inducted into the athletic hall of fame. She has a master of arts from the University of Nebraska Omaha, and her educational administrative endorsement and doctorate from the University of Nebraska–Lincoln.

Philip B. Warrick, EdD, spent the first twenty-five years of his education career as a teacher, assistant principal, principal, and superintendent and has experience in leading schools in the states of Nebraska and Texas. Dr. Warrick was named 1998 Nebraska Outstanding New Principal of the Year and was the 2005 Nebraska State High School Principal of the Year. He is a past regional president for the Nebraska Council of School Administrators (NCSA) and also served on the NCSA legislative committee. In 2003, he was one of the initial participants to attend the Nebraska Educational Leadership Institute, conducted by the Gallup Corporation at Gallup University in Omaha. In 2008, Dr. Warrick was hired as the campus principal at Round Rock High School in Round Rock, Texas. In 2010, he was invited to be an inaugural participant in the Texas Principals' Visioning Institute, where he collaborated with other principals from the state of Texas to develop a vision for effective practices in Texas schools.

Dr. Warrick joined the Solution Tree–Marzano Resources team in 2011 and works as an author and global consultant in the areas of school leadership, curriculum, instruction, assessment, grading, and collaborative teaming. Dr. Warrick has coauthored *A School Leader's Guide to Standards-Based Grading, Collaborative Teams That Transform Schools, A Handbook for High Reliability Schools,* and *Leading a High Reliability School*.

He earned a bachelor of science from Chadron State College in Chadron, Nebraska, and earned his master's and doctoral degrees from the University of Nebraska–Lincoln.

To book Jan K. Hoegh, Tammy Heflebower, or Philip B. Warrick for professional development, contact pd@MarzanoResources.com.

Foreword

by Robert J. Marzano

My colleague John Kendall and I first wrote about the concept of a proficiency scale in 1996 in a book titled *A Comprehensive Guide to Designing Standards-Based Districts, Schools, and Classrooms* (Marzano & Kendall, 1996). At that time, the concept of a proficiency scale was quite new and the version that we articulated was unique. It was the product of years of trial and error with various forms of such scales. If memory serves, we tried over a dozen versions before we settled on the one in the *Comprehensive Guide.*

One of the unique features of the scale is that it has only three levels of explicitly stated content. To create a scale, one begins with the content that is the target of instruction. When students demonstrate their understanding of the target content it signifies they are proficient at the topic for which the scale was created. The level of content below the target represents that information that is necessary to learn the target content and will be directly taught by the teacher. The level above the target content represents advanced inferences and applications relative to the target content. Surprisingly, it took a number of years to settle on this rather simple hierarchy but its simplicity is its strength. We found that teachers, regardless of the content or the grade level they taught, could resonate with identifying and using these three levels: target content, content necessary to learn the target content, and content that goes above and beyond the target.

Even adding one more level of explicit content to the hierarchy creates a complexity that makes the design and use of proficiency scales prohibitive.

With these three explicit levels of content identified, it is easy to add other levels that represent discernable benchmarks of understanding but do not require adding explicit content. One added level indicates that students have not demonstrated competence independently but can demonstrate some understanding with aid from the teacher. Another added level indicates that even with help students cannot demonstrate understanding of any of the content. Thus, the full scale in its generic form has five levels, each with a numeric code.

4.0: The student has demonstrated mastery of the content that goes beyond the target content.

3.0: The student has demonstrated mastery of the target content.

2.0: The student has demonstrated mastery of the content necessary to learn the target content.

1.0: With help, the student has demonstrated partial understanding of some of the content.

0.0: Even with help, the student has not demonstrated understanding of any content.

For purposes of measurement, half-point scores are added to the scale. For example, a score of 2.5 indicates that students understand all the content at the 2.0 level and have partial understanding of the content at the 3.0 level.

When a curriculum is articulated as topics (which we refer to as measurement topics), each of which is accompanied by a proficiency scale, students, teachers, administrators, and parents have a clear picture of what is expected at each grade level and each subject area. A well-articulated system of proficiency scales forms the foundation for highly effective instruction, assessment, grading, and reporting.

Since the publication of the *Comprehensive Guide* in 1996, proficiency scales have been used in every U.S. state and a number of other countries. Jan Hoegh, Tammy Heflebower, and Phil Warrick have done a great deal of the professional development to this end and have helped educators at all grade levels make adaptations and additions to proficiency scales that meet their specific needs. This handbook describes the myriad possible uses of proficiency scales that Hoegh and her colleagues have observed and helped generate. This handbook makes the design and use of proficiency scales easily understandable and accessible to all educators.

—Robert J. Marzano

Chief Academic Officer, Marzano Resources
Strategic Advisor, Marzano Research

Introduction

I can recall vividly the mid-1990s when academic standards gained prominence in the field of education. The intention of the standards movement was to more clearly define the knowledge and skills that students are expected to learn. However, this clarity often does not materialize—not for me back then, and not for many classroom teachers nearly thirty years later. Teachers struggle to use standards effectively to determine what students must know and be able to do. Textbooks and other curriculum resources continue to replace standards as the primary resource when planning and implementing classroom instruction. That was certainly the case for me as a classroom teacher for fourteen years.

The idea for proficiency scales came from my friend, colleague, and mentor Dr. Robert J. Marzano, with the goal of ensuring clarity about what students need to know and be able to do by the end of a grade level or course. A *proficiency scale* is a tool for describing a standard in a progression of knowledge. It provides information about the most critical knowledge and skills encompassed within a standard. Marzano wrote about scales in early publications, such as *Making Standards Useful in the Classroom* (Marzano & Haystead, 2008) and *Designing and Teaching Learning Goals and Objectives* (Marzano, 2009), and has continued to share his vast knowledge in numerous ways. Other authors and educators have furthered this work, in publications such as *A Teacher's Guide to Standards-Based Learning* (Heflebower, Hoegh, Warrick, & Flygare, 2019) and *The New Art and Science of Classroom Assessment* (Marzano, Norford, & Ruyle, 2019).

While a wealth of information about proficiency scales exists in print and online resources, teachers still find the task of writing proficiency scales challenging, and sometimes even overwhelming or daunting. Not only does scale development require deep knowledge of academic content, it takes significant time to ensure a high-quality end product. At the onset of scale development, it may be difficult for a teacher to envision how he or she will use scales in the classroom. This book addresses these and other scale-related challenges.

About This Book

This book is a comprehensive resource for teachers who use or want to use proficiency scales in their classrooms. Each chapter will address an essential topic related to developing and using scales. Chapter 1 defines proficiency scales and establishes why teachers should use them. Chapter 2 describes several practical methods that teachers can use to develop scales for their content. Chapter 3 takes a closer look at the advanced or more complex level of the scale (score 4.0), as it is often the most challenging level for a teacher team to determine. Chapter 4 describes how various stakeholder groups use and benefit from proficiency scales. Chapter 5 explores several tools that teachers may use in concert with scales, including rubrics, checklists, and pacing guides. Particular considerations for using proficiency scales with exceptional learners are the subject of chapter 6. Chapter 7 discusses scales for nonacademic content such as cognitive skills, self-management skills, and other behaviors that promote academic success. Comprehension questions appear at the end of each chapter to help readers solidify their understanding of the content. Finally, the appendices contain example scales for a variety of content areas and grade levels, as well as other reproducibles and tools. Throughout the book, readers will find a wealth of sample scales to illustrate the topics presented. I have collected these through my work with teachers, schools, and districts, who have generously shared their products in support of other educators. In its totality, this book contains everything you need to know in order to effectively employ proficiency scales in your classroom.

CHAPTER 1
The *What* and *Why* of Proficiency Scales

The role of classroom teacher seems to be synonymous with that of constant decision maker. Teachers are continually faced with decisions about how to teach or assess certain content, how to handle specific student behaviors, or which teaching resources are credible and which are not. These are just a few of the challenges commonly presented to a teacher that require decision making and problem solving in order to resolve a particular quandary. This book focuses on a challenge that began when standards became part of the educational environment.

Since the beginning of the standards era, teachers have faced the prevailing challenge of providing students with adequate opportunities in the instructional time available to learn the content encompassed within the standards. The struggle is real, as documented by researchers such as Robert Marzano and John Kendall, who quantified the amount of instructional time needed to teach the content of standards. Their conclusion was that we have far less instructional time available than teaching the standards demands (Marzano & Kendall, 1999).

As a result of the quandary presented to teachers by the magnitude of standards documents, educators have engaged in meaningful decision-making processes, such as identifying the most important content that all students must master. Larry

Ainsworth (2003) popularized this prioritization work in the early 21st century when he authored *Power Standards: Identifying the Standards That Matter Most*. From that point forward, many schools and districts have used various criteria (such as endurance, teacher judgment, and assessment value) to identify the standards that have a higher degree of importance than others (Ainsworth, 2003; Heflebower, Hoegh, & Warrick, 2014). While this prioritization work was and is a critical first step in the right direction toward achieving clarity about what students must know and be able to do, there are numerous related dilemmas it doesn't solve. Three are particularly salient to this book.

1. Will the teachers responsible for teaching the most important standards have a consistent understanding of the knowledge and skills contained within these standards?

2. Will students have a clear understanding of the knowledge and skills they need to demonstrate to show proficiency?

3. Will parents understand what their child needs to know and be able to do in a specific grade level or course?

The answers to these questions, as well as numerous others, are found in a proficiency scale.

What Is a Proficiency Scale?

A proficiency scale is a tool that displays a collection of related learning targets and scores for determining a student's current level of performance. In *A Teacher's Guide to Standards-Based Learning*, the authors stated that "a proficiency scale defines a learning progression or set of learning goals for a specific topic, relative to a given standard" (Heflebower et al., 2019, p. 8). Marzano (2006) described a scale as "a logical progression of understanding and skill for a specific measurement topic" (p. 41). This is a tool that shows teachers, students, and others what proficiency looks like, what knowledge and skills must be attained for mastery, and how students might go beyond what the standard requires. Figure 1.1 presents the generic form of a proficiency scale.

Score	Description
4.0	Complex content—a performance beyond what a standard requires
3.0	Target content—the level of learning required for all students
2.0	Simple content—basic knowledge or skill necessary for mastering the target content
1.0	With help, partial success with score 2.0 content and score 3.0 content
0.0	Even with help, no success

Source: Heflebower et al., 2019, p. 8.

Figure 1.1: The generic form of a proficiency scale.

When academic content replaces the generic descriptors (see examples in appendix A [page 101] and throughout this book), the proficiency scale becomes a powerful means of clarifying what students must know and be able to do by the end of an academic year or course.

A proficiency scale is first and foremost a tool for teachers and students, but it also serves parents. For teachers, the scale provides information regarding instruction, assessment, and feedback to the learner.

For students, the proficiency scale is the primary source of information about what they need to know and be able to do in relation to a priority standard or set of standards. Finally, a proficiency scale can serve as a source of information for parents. When a teacher, school, or district provides access to proficiency scales, parents are able to better understand the instructional focus of a content area or course.

As an example, consider the following priority standard for fourth-grade mathematics: "The student will compare two fractions with different numerators and different denominators using <, >, and =, and justify the comparison." Since the school or district has determined that this standard is very important—one that students absolutely must master by the end of the year—they also developed a proficiency scale to provide additional clarity regarding the knowledge and skills that students must demonstrate to be considered proficient. Figure 1.2 is a scale for the comparing fractions priority standard.

A teacher who uses this scale has information about vocabulary terms and basic facts (the score 2.0 content) that students need to understand during the opportunity to learn. Based on score 3.0, the teacher also has explicit information about what constitutes mastery of this standard. Most important, the teacher has a means of clearly communicating with students about what they need to learn in order to be proficient on comparing fractions.

Students can also use this tool in various ways. Students often use the scale to reflect on their current levels of performance. The thought process of a student engaging in this practice might sound like, "Right now, I know the vocabulary and the other basic processes at score 2.0, but I can't do everything at score 3.0. That is where I need to work in order to become proficient." The scale is then a resource that lists specific knowledge and skills that the student can target to improve performance.

NUMBER AND QUANTITY Comparing Fractions, Grade 4	
Score 4.0	In addition to score 3.0 performance, the student demonstrates in-depth inferences and applications that go beyond what was taught. • For example, given three or more fractions with different denominators, the student orders them least to greatest or greatest to least. • For example, the student compares improper and mixed fractions with unlike denominators.
Score 3.0	The student: • Compares two fractions with different numerators and different denominators using <, >, and = • Justifies the comparison
Score 2.0	The student recognizes or recalls specific vocabulary, such as: • *compare, comparison, denominator, equivalent, fraction, generate, justify, numerator* The student performs basic processes, such as: • Recognizing symbols, such as <, >, and = • Generating equivalent fractions • Comparing two fractions with like denominators
Score 1.0	With help, the student demonstrates partial success at score 2.0 and score 3.0.
Score 0.0	Even with help, the student demonstrates no understanding of the 2.0 and score 3.0 content.

Source: © 2019 by Clark-Pleasant Community School Corporation. Used with permission.

Figure 1.2: Scale for comparing fractions, grade 4.

For parents, this scale is only one part of the picture of what their children will learn in class. Consider that, in addition to the scale for comparing fractions, there are another twelve proficiency scales for fourth-grade mathematics. Parents of fourth-grade students in this school (or district) can examine all thirteen scales and gain a solid understanding of what their child needs to learn during the academic year. Providing access to the proficiency scales sets parents up to better support their children and to effectively communicate with the teacher when needed.

As expressed in our definition, everything on a proficiency scale is related. This idea is evident on the proficiency scale for comparing fractions. There is no mention of computation, metric conversion, or any other mathematics concept on this scale. The content at each level is closely related to the same topic (comparing fractions). Everything in the lower levels of the scale is an important step

toward attaining mastery. For example, in order for a student to become proficient on the comparing fractions scale, he or she must recognize <, >, and = symbols—clearly a basic learning target within the concept of comparing fractions.

In summary, a proficiency scale presents a learning progression related to a priority standard or topic (several related standards grouped together). To better understand the details of proficiency scales, we'll next explore more details about the levels of the scale, as well as a variety of scale formats.

Levels of the Scale

The scores on a proficiency scale are a very important feature for determining a student's level of mastery at any point in time during the opportunity to learn. Three types of content are represented on a proficiency scale by scores 2.0, 3.0, and 4.0—simple content, target content, and complex content, respectively. To understand these three types, consider the three learning targets from the comparing fractions example.

- **Score 4.0 (complex content):** Compares improper and mixed fractions with unlike denominators

- **Score 3.0 (target content):** Compares two fractions with different numerators and different denominators using <, >, and =

- **Score 2.0 (simple content):** Recognizes symbols, such as <, >, and =

The score 2.0 content "Recognizes symbols, such as <, >, and =" is *simple content*, or foundational knowledge that the student must possess in order to master the target content. Simple content is typically very basic, often related to vocabulary or declarative knowledge. Sometimes, simple content is a basic process that students must master before reaching the level of the priority standard. This basic content may have been target content in a previous grade level or course. Because it is important background knowledge, it is a learning target at score 2.0. Other times, simple content is a more basic version of the priority standard. On the comparing fractions scale, the score 2.0 learning target "Compares two fractions with like denominators" is the simpler version of the score 3.0 learning target "Compares two fractions with different numerators and different denominators using <, >, and =." Almost all proficiency scales include some academic vocabulary as part of score 2.0 because it is an essential type of background knowledge. In summary, the simple content prepares students to acquire mastery of the target content.

The *target content* on a proficiency scale is what all students must know and be able to do by the end of the year (or course). The content at this level aligns most closely to the priority standard; therefore, when a student demonstrates mastery of each target at score 3.0, he or she is considered proficient on the standard. It is important to note that the complexity of knowledge, cognition, or skill required of students at score 3.0 is greater than that required

of students at score 2.0. In the case of the comparing fractions scale, the target content includes two learning targets. A student must demonstrate mastery of both learning targets to be considered proficient on this scale.

The score 4.0 content is *complex content* that goes beyond the level of proficiency or course expectations. This content is not a requirement—not all students will reach score 4.0. If students demonstrate mastery of scores 2.0 and 3.0, however, they have the opportunity to engage in complex content activities. A defining feature of score 4.0 content is that students must apply the knowledge or skill acquired in previous levels. The cognition required of students at this level is more complex than the cognition required at score 3.0. Additionally, there are typically numerous ways that a student can demonstrate the ability to apply his or her knowledge of the target content. For that reason, score 4.0 learning targets often begin with the phrase "for example." More information is provided about score 4.0 on a proficiency scale in chapter 3 (page 31).

There are two additional levels on a proficiency scale that require explanation: score 0.0 and score 1.0. Academic content does not appear in either of these levels, but instead, generic descriptions of student performance. A student whose current level of performance is at score 1.0 is very early in the process of mastering the target content. So early, in fact, that he or she requires help when asked to demonstrate knowledge or skill. Examples of such help might include but are not limited to: repeating the question using different words; asking probing questions to activate the memory system; and using prompts or sentence starters related to the desired response. With such help, a student performing at score 1.0 can demonstrate partial understanding of the score 2.0 or score 3.0 content.

The definition of score 0.0 is that the student is unable to demonstrate any understanding of the score 2.0 or score 3.0 content, despite receiving help. This will be a rare occasion, as long as the student participates in the learning opportunities provided and receives various types of support. Since teachers will not assign a score 0.0 very frequently, some may decide that it isn't necessary to display on the proficiency scales they use in the classroom.

One final idea is essential to understanding the levels on a proficiency scale. Some scale users like to include half-point increments (0.5, 1.5, 2.5, 3.5). In fact, we encourage this practice, as it allows more specificity regarding a student's current level of performance. For example, consider a student who can perform everything at score 2.0, and some of the requirements of score 3.0. A score of 2.5 most accurately represents the student's current level of knowledge and skill. For students who struggle to gain adequate knowledge to move up an entire score level (for example, from 2.0 to 3.0), the half-point increment allows them and their teachers to see and document their growth. Figure 1.3 presents an expanded version of the generic form of a proficiency scale presented earlier in this chapter (page 4), including the half-point increments.

Formats for Scales

In our definitions of proficiency scales so far, we have not made any statements about a specific format for the scale. There is no single correct format for proficiency scales. Having said this, there will be some similarity across possible scale formats, given that the scale must articulate a progression of knowledge. The decision about format really rests on the preferences of the teacher or team of teachers that eventually will use the scale. Some teachers prefer the academic content displayed vertically while others prefer a horizontal format. Sometimes scale developers choose to include descriptive language related to the scale levels while others only include language related to the academic content. Some scales present sample activities or even instructional supports for specific subgroups of students in addition to the progression of knowledge. There is not a right or wrong format as long as it is the result of thought about what makes sense and will work well for the users.

The following examples (figure 1.4, page 8, figure 1.5, page 8, and figure 1.6, page 11) are all possible formats for proficiency scales, and are different from what has been presented in this book up to this point. Regardless of the format, each scale clearly defines a sequence of knowledge, skill, and content. Appendix B (page 129) contains several common templates for proficiency scales, along with content-specific examples for each.

Score 4.0	In addition to score 3.0 performance, the student demonstrates in-depth inferences and applications that go beyond what was taught.
Score 3.5	In addition to score 3.0 performance, partial success with score 4.0 content
Score 3.0	Target content or level of mastery required for all students
Score 2.5	No major errors or omissions regarding score 2.0 content and partial success with score 3.0 content
Score 2.0	Simple content or basic knowledge and skill necessary for mastery of the target content
Score 1.5	Partial success with score 2.0 content and major errors or omissions regarding score 3.0 content
Score 1.0	With help, partial success with score 2.0 content and score 3.0 content
Score 0.5	With help, partial success with score 2.0 content but not with score 3.0 content
Score 0.0	Even with help, no success

Source: Adapted from Heflebower et al., 2014, p. 26.

Figure 1.3: Generic form of the proficiency scale with half-point scores.

READING COMPREHENSION: ENGLISH 9

Students will construct meaning by applying prior knowledge, using text information, and monitoring comprehension while reading increasingly complex grade-level literary and informational text.

Analyze and evaluate the relationships between elements of literary text.	Summarize, analyze, and synthesize the themes and main ideas between a literary and informational work.	Construct and answer literal, inferential, critical, and interpretive questions, analyzing and synthesizing evidence from the text and additional sources to support answers.

4.0: Complex content

For example, a student may:

- Assess the impact of prior knowledge, such as author's purpose or historical background and compare the novel to another piece of literature (for example, the importance of the World War II setting to both *The Chosen* and *Red Sky at Morning*)
- Compare and contrast the effects of different plot points on the outcome of the novel

3.0: Target content

Analyze the relationships between elements of literary text.	Analyze the themes and main ideas between a literary and informational work.	Construct and answer questions, analyzing evidence from the text and additional sources to support answers.

2.0: Simple content

Define critical vocabulary, such as: *characterization, conflict, mood, plot, setting, theme, tone.*	Identify the theme and main idea in both literary and informational work.	Answer questions that are teacher provided in relation to a literary or informational text.

1.0: Help needed from the teacher to demonstrate knowledge at score 2.0 or score 3.0

Source: © 2019 by Columbus Public Schools. Used with permission.

Figure 1.4: Scale for reading comprehension in a ninth-grade English class.

Seventh-Grade Choir Proficiency Scale

Student Name:

Date:

Performance Assessment (circle one): Beginning   Middle   End

	Score 4.0 Advanced	Score 3.0 Proficient	Score 2.0 Progressing	Score 1.0 Beginning
Performance Category 1: **Singing Technique**	• I can apply tone qualities to different characters in a musical production. • I can compare and contrast bright and dark tones among professional performers and themselves.	• I can perform using correct singing technique in performance and rehearsal (for example, pitch, tone quality, breath support, posture).	• I can describe correct singing technique in performance and rehearsal (for example, pitch, tone quality, breath support, posture). • I can respond to correct singing technique in others (for example, journal entry, checklist, dialogue).	• With help, I can do score 2.0.

Your Rating and Reason: **Teacher Rating:**				
Performance Category 2: **Solfege and Note Names**	• I can decipher other key signatures based on the key signature formula. • I can apply solfege to the key of the concert music.	• I can perform a two-measure melodic line in my clef using solfege and note names in the key of C in a small-group setting.	• I can define vocabulary words, such as: *accidental*, *flat*, *key signature*, *natural*, *sharp*. • I can identify lines and spaces of treble clef or bass clef using ledger lines. • I can identify solfege major scale syllables with the notes on the staff in the key of C. • I can identify the key of C in concert music.	• With help, I can do score 2.0.
Your Rating and Reason: **Teacher Rating:**				
Performance Category 3: **Rhythmic Notation**	• I can determine score 2.0 rhythms located in concert music. • I can infer how higher-level rhythms will be sight read based on my skills in score 2.0.	• I can perform a sight-reading rhythm using complex eighth note variations in common time. • I can create two measures of rhythmic notation in common time.	• I can identify rhythmic notation for whole, half, quarter, eighth, and dotted notes and in variations in common time. • I can write out rhythmic notations of given examples.	• With help, I can do score 2.0.
Your Rating and Reason: **Teacher Rating:**				

Figure 1.5: Scale for grade 7 choir.

continued ⇨

Performance Category 4: Expression	• I can analyze intended emotion of a song outside of my concert music. • I can compare two different performances of the same song and describe the ensemble's expression of intended emotion in each performance.	• I can express the intended emotion of concert music with appropriate facial expression, body movement, dynamics, phrasing, and articulation.	• I can define vocabulary words, such as: *articulation*, *dynamics*, *intended emotion*, *phrase*. • I can explain the composer's intended emotion of a song through lyrics, key, phrasing, and melodic line. • I can find phrasing in the melodic lines of concert music. • I can describe how to use my body to show intended emotion while I sing.	• With help, I can do score 2.0.
Your Rating and Reason: **Teacher Rating:**				
Performance Category 5: Rehearsal and Performance Etiquette	• I can teach the rehearsal and performance etiquette to peers. • I can propose suggestions for performance etiquette that may improve the overall performance of the group.	• I can demonstrate proper musician etiquette in rehearsal and performance. • I can describe how musician rehearsal and performance etiquette is achieved using focus, encouragement, goal setting, and following classroom procedures.	• I can classify actions that demonstrate focus on the director. • I can recite rehearsal procedures. • I can state the three choir commitments (to the music, to the individual, and to the choir).	• With help, I can do score 2.0.
Your Rating and Reason: **Teacher Rating:**				

Source: © 2019 by Columbus Public Schools. Used with permission.

FOUNDATIONS OF GOVERNMENT
Students will analyze and evaluate the foundation, structures, and functions of the U.S. government as well as local, state, and international governments.
Score 4.0
Students will: • Infer how our current government would be viewed by the founders of the U.S. government
Score 3.0
Students will: • Develop conclusions about the best types of government • Analyze America's founding documents • Describe the intended meaning of the word *state* • Understand the evolution of the political process
Score 2.0
Students will: • Recognize or recall specific terminology, such as: *Declaration of Independence, English Bill of Rights, Magna Carta, Petition of Right, public policy* • State the basic purpose of government • Compare and contrast the different types of government (for example, capitalism, democracy, dictatorship, monarchy, oligarchy) • Identify America's founding documents
Score 1.0
With help, students will demonstrate partial knowledge of 2.0 content.

Source: © 2019 by Columbus Public Schools. Used with permission.

Figure 1.6: Scale on the topic of foundations of government.

Why Are Proficiency Scales Important?

Having defined and described what a proficiency scale is, we will discuss why scales are so valuable. There are three primary reasons it is important for teachers to develop and use proficiency scales.

1. Proficiency scales serve as the basis for instruction in a standards-based classroom.

2. Proficiency scales serve as the framework for high-quality classroom assessment practices.

3. Proficiency scales present a means for offering meaningful feedback to learners about current levels of performance on a priority standard or topic.

The following sections will provide information and examples for each reason. For additional information about these three reasons, consult *A Teacher's Guide to Standards-Based Learning* (Heflebower et al., 2019).

As a Basis for Instruction

The development of proficiency scales is typically based on identifying the content that is most critical for students to master, as described earlier in this chapter. Because of the importance of this content, scales become the focus for instruction. In classrooms where scales are used optimally, a majority of instructional time is spent on teaching the simple and target content (and complex content when appropriate) that make up the knowledge progressions on proficiency scales. A teacher will also teach some content not represented on a proficiency scale, but it will be a smaller percentage of instructional time than that related to content on a scale.

It is very common for a teacher or team of teachers to develop twelve to fifteen proficiency scales for a single content area or course to be taught across an academic year or for the duration of the course. In the primary grades, the number of scales may be less and in advanced-level courses the number may be higher, but the range of twelve to fifteen is a helpful guide. Figure 1.7 is an example that displays the total number of proficiency scales per grade level and course, kindergarten through high school, for English language arts and mathematics.

Once proficiency scales are in place, a teacher or a team of teachers can determine the most logical progression for teaching the content on the scales. The order for teaching content is often based on the teacher's primary curriculum resource—that is, a textbook. Scales don't replace textbooks, but they are valuable in that they inform teachers about how to use this primary curriculum resource in the most appropriate and impactful way possible (Heflebower

Grade Level		ELA	Mathematics
Kindergarten		12	11
First		13	12
Second		14	10
Third		14	14
Fourth		13	11
Fifth		10	11
Sixth		9	10
Seventh		15	12
Eighth		11	8
Ninth-Grade Literature and Composition	Algebra 1	9	13
Tenth-Grade Literature and Composition	Algebra 2	14	10

Source: © 2019 by Fulton County Schools. Used with permission.

Figure 1.7: Number of proficiency scales for ELA and mathematics at each grade level.

et al., 2014). Textbooks commonly include content not required by standards. When proficiency scales are the basis for instruction, a teacher can align curriculum materials to each proficiency scale. Figure 1.8 is an example of how a team of science teachers completed this process. Note that there are gaps in the table, which represent the need for additional curriculum resources.

	Scale 1: Climate and Weather	Scale 2: Force and Motion	Scale 3: Electricity	Scale 4: Comparing Organisms	Scale 5: Organism Behaviors
Chapter	1	4	6	3	3
Score 4.0	--	Page 69	--	--	--
Score 3.0	Pages 15–18	Pages 56–63	Pages 95–100	Pages 38–40	--
Score 2.0	Pages 7–12	Pages 52–55	Pages 88–92	Pages 33–35	Pages 46–47

Source: Adapted from Heflebower et al., 2014, p. 34.

Figure 1.8: Curriculum materials alignment.

In addition to defining curriculum, each individual proficiency scale provides instructional information for the classroom teacher. Since score 2.0 on the scale presents simple content—background knowledge—it makes sense that a teacher would start instruction on a topic at this score level. He or she can plan and deliver lessons based on the score 2.0 learning targets. Once the teacher is confident that students have acquired the necessary background knowledge to learn the target content, he or she can progress instruction to the score 3.0 level. We'll explore instruction based on scales in more detail in chapter 4 (page 43).

At times, it will be necessary to differentiate instruction based on how individual students perform relative to the learning targets at each score level. There may be times when some students are working on the learning targets at score 2.0, some at 3.0, and maybe even a few students at score 4.0. When proficiency scales serve as the basis for instruction, differentiation occurs more easily, as described in the following classroom vignette.

Mrs. Jorgenson is about to begin teaching the grade 4 instructional unit for comparing fractions. She knows that students will have some background knowledge, as fractions are a priority in third grade in her school. She spends the first class period going over the comparing fractions proficiency scale. She can tell by some students' reactions to the content on the scale that they are excited about the upcoming unit. Other students appear concerned, and some seem neutral. After presenting the proficiency scale for the unit, she begins to address the learning targets at score 2.0. It is obvious to her that most members of her class are comfortable with the <, >, and = symbols. When she reviews comparing fractions with like denominators, the majority of students do extremely well. While she is pleased with how well most students demonstrate understanding of the necessary background knowledge,

she notes four students who needed a lot of support on the content covered during this initial lesson. As she plans for the math lesson the next day, she determines that it is necessary to establish two flexible groups—one that consists of the majority of the class and one that is made up of those four students who need additional review. She knows that if she keeps all her students together in one group, the four students who need significant support will struggle going forward.

The next day, she establishes the two groups. While she supports the four students for about ten minutes, she has the other students work with a partner to complete an activity related to the score 2.0 targets. Once she gets the four students started on the same activity, Mrs. Jorgenson provides instruction to the majority of the class on generating equivalent fractions. Her goal is to tailor her teaching to each group's current level of understanding to provide instruction that will eventually get both groups to approximately the same place on the scale. Until that is the case, she will differentiate instruction through the use of flexible groups.

As a Framework for Assessment

Just as proficiency scales guide instruction, they inform classroom assessment practices. Each learning target on a proficiency scale represents a statement of intended knowledge gain for students. The only way a teacher knows whether or not this intended knowledge gain has occurred is by assessing learners. A teacher may choose to assess learners formally or informally. In fact, in *The New Art and Science of Teaching*, Marzano (2017) discussed formal and informal assessment: "At its core, assessment is a feedback mechanism for students and teachers. Assessments should provide students with information about how to advance their understanding of content and teachers with information about how to help students do so" (p. 21).

Regardless of the type of assessment, it is important for the teacher to know whether or not students have mastered each of the individual learning targets on a scale. In essence, the language on the proficiency scale drives the assessment practices that are implemented. Consider figure 1.9, which displays how a teacher might assess progress for each learning target in the comparing fractions proficiency scale.

As a Means for Offering Feedback

Much has been written in educational literature about the importance of meaningful feedback. Different researchers have provided varying lists of attributes of effective feedback. For example, Grant Wiggins (2012) said that helpful feedback is goal-referenced, tangible and transparent, actionable, user-friendly, timely, ongoing, and consistent. In 2011, John Hattie wrote about feedback in schools in the book *Feedback: The Communication of Praise, Criticism, and Advice*:

There are a number of conditions necessary for feedback to be received and have a positive effect. There needs to be transparent and challenging goals (learning intentions), and an understanding of a student's current status relative to these goals. It is best if the criteria of success are transparent and understood, and that the student has commitment and skills in investing and implementing strategies as well as understandings relative to these goals and success criteria. (pp. 11–12)

No doubt, there are additional researchers and attributes of effective feedback we could cite. For the purpose of this discussion, let's assume that most educators agree that effective feedback is timely, specific, and corrective. Scales provide a means to ensure that feedback is effective by making plausible the manifestation of all three of those attributes.

Consider figure 1.9 again. Following the administration of any of the assessment practices noted,

	Learning Target	Assessment Example
Score 4.0	Orders three fractions with different numerators and denominators and explains the process he or she used	Order the following three fractions from least to greatest. Then explain how you made your decision. $$\frac{6}{8} \qquad \frac{4}{9} \qquad \frac{5}{10}$$
Score 3.0	Compares two fractions with different numerators and different denominators using <, >, and =	Provide each student with five notecards, each displaying two fractions. Ask the student to insert the correct symbol between the two fractions.
	Justifies the comparison	Randomly choose one of the five notecards given to the student. Ask him or her to justify why he chose the symbol.
Score 2.0	Recognizes symbols, such as <, >, and =	Ask students to complete a set of five items where they insert the correct symbol between two numbers (for example, 12 < 15, 25 = 20 + 5, 100 > 10).
	Generates equivalent fractions	Provide manipulatives for students to use to generate an equivalent fraction to a teacher-provided fraction.
	Compares two fractions with like denominators	Provide a worksheet comprised of ten fraction pairs, all having like denominators. Students insert the appropriate symbol to accurately represent the comparison.

Source: Adapted from Heflebower et al., 2019, p. 74.

Figure 1.9: Assessment examples for comparing fractions.

it would be quite easy to offer the student meaningful feedback in a timely manner. Let's consider the learning target "Compare two fractions with like denominators." Once a student completes the fill-in-the-blank assessment aligned to that target, the teacher can give verbal or written feedback focused on that target. For example, imagine that Justine completed ten items on a fill-in-the-blank assessment, but only used the appropriate symbol on four of ten fraction pairs. At that point, the teacher is able to offer feedback that is clear, specific, and corrective:

Justine, you are on your way to demonstrating mastery of this learning target. You got four of ten items correct! You clearly understand the equals symbol. However, you seem to be confused about the less than and greater than symbols. Let's work together to ensure you gain understanding of both, because it is critical that you master this target.

With such feedback, the student has clarity about where she must exert attention and effort for improvement.

As another example, if a student is able to insert the correct symbol between the two fractions with different numerators and denominators but is not able to justify why the symbol was chosen, it is quite easy for a teacher to offer feedback. The teacher might say:

It is clear that you understand the symbols <, >, and =. However, you are still working toward mastery of explaining why your choice of the symbol is correct. Let's work together to ensure you master this learning target as well.

When proficiency scales are used to drive instruction and assessment, feedback aligns more closely with learning and assessment tasks. This version of learning makes sense to students, as everything is clearly connected. When this is the case, students' goals seem attainable, which may ultimately be a primary factor in producing higher levels of student achievement.

Summary

This chapter presented information about what proficiency scales are and why they are important. A proficiency scale is a valuable tool that has implications for every aspect of learning. Scales provide valuable information for teachers regarding instruction of important content. Scales also guide formal and informal classroom assessment practices. Finally, proficiency scales provide a means for giving students valuable and meaningful feedback. When scales are made available to learners and parents, it is easier for them to understand the expectations for learning in a grade level or course. We'll conclude this chapter by reiterating three key points associated with proficiency scales.

1. A proficiency scale communicates priority content, which means that the content is explicitly taught and assessed.

2. A proficiency scale articulates a learning progression related to a priority standard or topic.

3. A proficiency scale allows students to reflect on their learning and track their progress.

The remaining chapters will discuss how to develop proficiency scales and how to use them effectively in the classroom.

Chapter 1 Comprehension Questions

1. What is a proficiency scale?

2. What is important to know about simple content, target content, and complex content?

3. Why are proficiency scales important?

4. What are some different uses for proficiency scales?

CHAPTER 2
Proficiency Scale Development

Now that we have established what a proficiency scale is and why proficiency scales are important, it is appropriate to focus on how to develop them. There are multiple ways to address this task. This chapter will describe four methods for developing scales, approaches for adapting existing scales, and guidance for unique situations. All of these are acceptable ways for individual teachers, collaborative teams, schools, and districts to build a set of these important tools.

Methods for Creating Your Own Scales

Teachers or school teams may decide to create their own scales, and there are several reasons they might do so. First, when a teacher or team of teachers develops proficiency scales, the process fosters ownership of the scales as valuable classroom tools. A second positive effect of scale development is deeper content expertise as a result of careful examination of standards and meaningful, focused conversation—both of which are components of the scale development process. Finally, when the primary users of the scales (teachers) develop the scales themselves, they have self-generated critical information about what students need to know and be able to do.

Four methods of scale development include:

1. Using a standard as score 3.0 content

2. Using a five-step process to determine score levels

3. Identifying individual learning targets within a standard

4. Writing a scale based on a topic

The following sections present these methods from least to most sophisticated. Appendix C (page 141) contains checklists for scale development.

It is important to note that all four methods approach the content starting with score 3.0, then determining score 2.0, and finally filling in score 4.0. This consistent approach to developing proficiency scales is purposeful, as the target content (expectation for all students) is the basis for the entire learning progression. Thus, scale developers should determine score 3.0 first—before addressing either the simple or complex content.

Using a Standard as Score 3.0 Content

Since a priority standard is a statement of knowledge or skill that students must master by the end of the year, it makes sense that it would be the focus of a proficiency scale. This approach to creating a scale is fairly simple in that the standard becomes the target (score 3.0) content without any modification or analysis. This is often the initial scale development method used by a teacher or team of teachers, as it is the most time-efficient methodology. This method works very well when scale users already understand the knowledge and skills encompassed within standards and there is minimal need to unpack the standards into more easily understood learning targets.

This method of scale development involves the following steps.

1. Record the priority standard in score 3.0 on the scale.

2. Determine critical vocabulary and other simple content and record it in score 2.0 on the scale.

3. Record a generic descriptor of score 4.0 on the scale.

Figure 2.1 is an example of what a scale might look like when developed through this method. A Common Core mathematics standard for addition appears in its entirety at score 3.0 (National Governors Association Center for Best Practices & Council of Chief State School Officers [NGA & CCSSO], 2010b). The simple content (score 2.0) evolved in response to the following question: What knowledge and skill must be in place to increase the likelihood of students mastering the target content (score 3.0)? As is evidenced in the scale, the teacher decided that some academic vocabulary is necessary for learners. These are words that the teacher will likely use as he or she teaches the content, as well as words learners may see in print as they begin learning the content. The other two learning targets at score 2.0 are foundational skills encompassed within the priority standard (target content).

When a school team uses this method, the number of priority standards and the number of proficiency scales will be the same. Teachers often like this approach because it is so logical—each

Score 4.0	In addition to score 3.0 performance, the student demonstrates in-depth inferences and applications that go beyond what was taught.
Score 3.0	The student will: Use addition to find the total number of objects arranged in rectangular arrays with up to five rows and up to five columns; write an equation to express the total as a sum of equal addends (2.OA.4)
Score 2.0	The student will recognize or recall specific vocabulary, such as: *addend, column, equation, member, rectangular array, row* The student will perform basic processes, such as: Recognize symbols, such as +, −, and = Determine whether a group of objects (up to 20) has an odd or even number of members; if the total is even, write an equation to express the total as a sum of two equal addends
Score 1.0	With help, partial success at score 2.0 content and score 3.0 content
Score 0.0	Even with help, no success

Source: Adapted from Marzano, Yanoski, Hoegh, & Simms, 2013, p. 217.

Figure 2.1: A mathematics scale that uses a standard as score 3.0 content.

priority standard evolves into its own proficiency scale. Moreover, there isn't any additional work to determining score 3.0, as the standard becomes the language at that level.

While using a standard as score 3.0 content is an acceptable method of development, it is not as specific as the other methods. Score 4.0 is typically just a generic description of a student performance, with no specific example provided. In order to overcome this lack of specificity at score 4.0, a teacher would have to take the additional step of defining some example activities (more information about score 4.0 appears in chapter 3). This method also potentially presents a challenge for precisely determining a student's current level of performance because standards often include multiple distinct elements or separate learning targets. In relation to the sample scale in figure 2.1, imagine a student who is able to "use addition to find the total number of objects arranged in rectangular arrays with up to five rows and up to five columns," but isn't able to "write an equation to express the total as a sum of equal addends (2.OA.4)." This student would receive a score of 2.0 (or 2.5, if half-point scores are in use), even though he has achieved one of the learning goals. A score of 2.0 doesn't seem as accurate as we might like, and yet is the most accurate we can be when considering what the student knows or is able to do in relation to the standard.

Using a Five-Step Process to Determine Score Levels

The second method we will discuss is using a five-step process to determine all three levels of the scale. This method of developing proficiency scales often works very well because it presents a concrete, step-by-step means of developing a well-constructed learning progression based on a prioritized standard. This method is also somewhat more comprehensive than simply using the standard as score 3.0 content. If scale developers aim to have single-idea statements of intended knowledge gain at each level (scores 2.0, 3.0, and 4.0), this method typically works quite well.

The steps included in this method are as follows.

1. Determine the topic of the proficiency scale.

2. Determine the language of score 3.0 (the target content).

3. Determine vocabulary related to the target content and record it in score 2.0.

4. Determine additional simple content and record it in score 2.0.

5. Identify an example or two of how a student might demonstrate a score 4.0 performance (the complex content).

As an example, consider this Common Core grade 2 mathematics standard: "The student will solve word problems with money using dollar bills, quarters, dimes, nickels, and pennies, using dollar and cents symbols appropriately" (NGA & CCSSO, 2010b, 2.MD.8). The following thought process demonstrates how a teacher would respond to each step in this five-step method.

1. **Determine the topic of the proficiency scale:** "While this standard is about money, it is more specific than that. It is about solving word problems with money. Let's call this proficiency scale 'Word Problems With Money.'"

2. **Determine the language of score 3.0:** "The language of the standard works well for this level, except it seems that using the dollar and cents symbols is prerequisite knowledge and skill. Let's move that portion of the standard down to score 2.0 on our scale. Score 3.0 will state 'The student will solve word problems with money using dollar bills, quarters, dimes, nickels, and pennies.'"

3. **Determine vocabulary related to the target content and record it in score 2.0:** "There are some critical terms that we will need to include on this scale, such as *all together, coin, decimal, remaining,* and *value.* There may be others we need to teach as well, but these are the terms we will record at score 2.0."

4. **Determine additional simple content and record it in score 2.0:** "We already have using the dollar and cents symbols correctly as part of score 2.0. Students will also definitely need to know each of the named coins and their values. Further, they will need to be able to add or subtract different coins to determine a total amount of money or money remaining. These additional

prerequisites will position students well for attaining mastery of score 3.0."

5. **Identify an example or two of how a student might demonstrate a score 4.0 performance:** "There are numerous ways a student could demonstrate a performance at this level, but what could a student do if he or she is able to solve word problems with dollar bills, quarters, dimes, nickels, and pennies? Let's have the student apply that knowledge by creating his or her own word problem, and let's go beyond a single-step problem."

As a result of this mental processing, the proficiency scale in figure 2.2 emerges.

A real benefit to this method of scale development is that the same sequence of steps is followed in order to develop each proficiency scale, creating a consistent process. Also, this method allows for the prioritized standard to be broken down into distinct elements, which is appropriate when parts of a standard are actually prerequisite knowledge and skill. In the case of the word problems with money standard, one part of the standard moved down to score 2.0 because the developers determined it to be simple content.

Identifying Individual Learning Targets Within a Standard

Many of the standards that students are expected to master are comprehensive statements of intended knowledge gain. In fact, when we thoroughly examine standards documents, it is quite easy to discern that a single standard is often comprised of multiple learning targets, or numerous distinct statements of knowledge or skill. When this is the case, a teacher can use the approach of identifying individual learning targets within a standard and then assigning each target to the appropriate level of the scale.

For example, consider the following grade 3 social studies standard: "The student will explain that governments provide certain types of goods and services in a market economy, and pay for these through taxes; describe services such as schools, libraries, roads, police/fire protection, and military" (Georgia Standards of Excellence, SS3E2; Georgia Department of Education, 2019). This standard encompasses multiple ideas. To begin the process, the teacher or team should identify the individual learning targets included in the standard. In the case of this social studies standard, a third-grade team might break down the standard into the following learning targets.

Score 4.0	The student will: • Write, solve, and share a multistep word problem involving dollar bills, quarters, dimes, nickels, and pennies
Score 3.0	The student will: • Solve word problems involving dollar bills, quarters, dimes, nickels, and pennies
Score 2.0	The student will: • Recognize or recall specific terminology, such as: *all together, coin, decimal, remaining, value* • Use $ and ¢ appropriately • Identify coins and their values • Add or subtract different coins to determine how much money all together or remaining
Score 1.0	With help, partial success at score 2.0 content and score 3.0 content

Source: Adapted from Marzano et al., 2013, p. 264.

Figure 2.2: Sample scale for word problems with money.

- Explain the certain types of goods and services the government provides in a market economy.
- Describe how the services (for example, schools, libraries, roads, police and fire protection, military) are supported through the payment of taxes.
- Define *economy*, *good*, *service*, *taxes*.
- Distinguish between a good and a service by categorizing examples of each.

Once the process of identifying learning targets within a standard is complete, the teachers can fairly easily assign each target to a score level on the proficiency scale. In the case of the grade 3 social studies standard, the scale-level assignments might result in the proficiency scale in figure 2.3.

The only level on the proficiency scale that isn't addressed in this approach is score 4.0—by definition, score 4.0 content goes beyond the expectations of the standard. However, with score 2.0 and 3.0 content in place, teachers typically create score 4.0 content without too much difficulty, especially when a team collaborates to write the example tasks for complex content (see chapter 3, page 31).

Writing a Scale Based on a Topic

When there are multiple standards that are taught interdependently (during the same unit of instruction), it makes sense to write a proficiency scale that is topic based. For example, consider the middle school mathematics proficiency scale for a unit of instruction on equations and inequalities in figure 2.4 (page 22). Multiple standards are included on this proficiency scale, as they are all closely related and part of a single instructional unit. In fact, some standards actually serve as prerequisite knowledge and skill for other standards and therefore become score 2.0 on the scale. As was the case in previous methods for scale development, teachers must determine the score 4.0 content by exemplifying complex applications of the content within the standards.

In order to ensure success with this method, use the following steps.

1. Identify standards that are taught within the same unit of instruction.
2. Determine the order in which the standards are taught.
3. Determine whether individual standards need to be unpacked into multiple single-idea learning targets.

Score 4.0	The student will: • Infer and describe what the country would be like if the government did not collect taxes
Score 3.0	The student will: • Explain the certain types of goods and services the government provides in a market economy • Describe how the services (for example, schools, libraries, roads, police and fire protection, military) are supported through the payment of taxes
Score 2.0	The student will: • Recognize or recall specific terminology, such as: *economy, good, service, taxes* • Distinguish between a good and a service by categorizing examples of each
Score 1.0	With help, partial success at score 2.0 content and score 3.0 content

Source: © 2019 by Fulton County Schools. Used with permission.

Figure 2.3: Social studies scale developed by identifying leveled content within a standard.

OPERATIONS AND ALGEBRA **Equations and Inequalities, Grade 6**	
Score 4.0	In addition to score 3.0 performance, the student demonstrates in-depth inferences and applications that go beyond what was taught. For example: • Write two-step algebraic equations to solve real-world problems • Solve problems that lead to compound inequalities
Score 3.0	The student will: • Solve real-world and mathematical equations of the form $x + p = q$ and $px = q$ when all variables are non-negative, rational numbers (6.EE.7) • Write an inequality of the form $x > c$ or $x < c$ to represent a constraint or condition of a real-world or mathematical problem (6.EE.8)
Score 2.0	The student will recognize or recall specific vocabulary, such as: • *condition, constraint, equation, expression, inequality, negative, rational number, variable* The student will perform basic processes, such as: • Use substitution to determine whether a given number makes an equation or inequality true (6.EE.5) • Use variables to represent numbers and write expressions (6.EE.6) • Represent solutions of inequalities on number line diagrams (6.EE.8)
Score 1.0	With help, partial success at score 2.0 content and score 3.0 content
Score 0.0	Even with help, no success

Source: Adapted from Marzano et al., 2013, p. 223; NGA & CCSSO, 2010b.

Figure 2.4: Topic-based proficiency scale that addresses multiple standards.

4. Make decisions about which level on the proficiency scale (score 2.0 or score 3.0) is most appropriate for each standard or learning target.

5. Generate a score 4.0 learning target for the proficiency scale.

The scale in figure 2.4 is an example of related standards being on the same proficiency scale. A teacher may use this scale to guide a few weeks of instruction and assessment. It is important to note that each learning target on the scale is a single-idea statement.

While scale development is significant and can seem overwhelming, it should be reassuring to teachers and leaders that there are numerous effective approaches to developing a proficiency scale. The four methods discussed here are all equally valid; in fact, it is perfectly fine to use more than one of these methods (or even all four) within a school or district. As long as the end result is a set of tools that display learning progressions for the most important standards, the method chosen for development doesn't matter. What matters is the resulting clarity about what all students must know and be able to do.

The following vignette explains one school's scale development process.

North Acadia Community Schools began the work of identifying priority standards and developing proficiency scales in 2013. In order to support this important work, the district hired an expert from Marzano Resources, who provided training about proficiency scales for a team of preschool through twelfth-grade teachers known as the district curriculum council. Following the initial training, the consultant supported teacher teams as they worked collaboratively to develop scales and later to revise their scales. At the beginning of the scale development process, the teacher teams were trained using the five-step process for determining score levels (page 19). Additionally, the curriculum council determined that all teachers would use the same scale format for districtwide consistency.

North Acadia educators spent the majority of an academic year developing proficiency scales. Teacher teams followed the guidance of twelve to fifteen scales per grade level or course for each content area, although some ended up with fewer than twelve scales in certain grade levels or courses, and more than fifteen scales in a few. Teachers then used these first drafts of the scales in their classrooms for the purpose of clearly communicating to students what they needed to know and be able to do.

As teachers piloted these newly developed proficiency scales, the curriculum council asked them to capture ideas for making revisions to the scales. The revision took place in June following the first year of scale implementation. Notes about the scales that teachers had captured throughout the year guided the necessary revisions to the scales. The end product of the June work was a set of enhanced proficiency scales that were ready to be implemented in classrooms in the following academic year. From that point forward, proficiency scale revision occurred at the end of each school year. North Acadia educators understand that scale development is an ongoing process and that there is always room for scales to get better.

Since developing proficiency scales, student performance on state tests has improved markedly across grade levels and content

areas. Educators from the school district commonly make the claim that this improved performance is, in part, related to the clarity that has resulted from their proficiency scale development. Teresa Elder, a district leader, reflected on the proficiency scale process, "Everything that happens in classrooms in this district is better as a result of proficiency scales. While it has taken numerous years to arrive to where we are now, I am confident in saying that very few teachers in this district would want to teach again without scales because of the clarity they provide for teachers, students, and parents. If North Acadia can do this, any district can!" (T. Elder, personal communication, June 6, 2018)

Adaptations of Existing Scales

Because of the potential amount of time it may take a teacher, team, school, or district to develop proficiency scales, they might decide to adopt and adapt scales created by others. There are many online resources, books, and other products available to educators who choose this option. Regardless of the source, it is essential to adapt others' scales to your unique needs and circumstances before using them in the classroom.

Teachers and schools commonly share the scales they have created through their own websites or online clearing houses for teacher-created resources. Scales created by other educators for your subject areas and grade levels make an excellent reference or starting point. There are also professionally developed scales for specific sets of standards. For example, *Using Common Core Standards to Enhance Classroom Instruction and Assessment* (Marzano et al., 2013) communicates a wealth of information about the Common Core State Standards and provides related proficiency scales for each of the standards. Similarly, *Proficiency Scales for the*

New Science Standards: A Framework for Science Instruction and Assessment (Marzano & Yanoski, 2016) provides commentary and scales based on the Next Generation Science Standards. As mentioned previously, adaptation is key—the scales in these books are "starter scales." In other words, a teacher or team of teachers could begin their scale development process with existing tools and work to improve them before using them in their own classrooms or buildings.

As another option, the Critical Concepts are a set of predeveloped proficiency scales that define a viable K–12 curriculum. Marzano Resources analysts, led by Julia Simms, identified priority measurement topics for the four core content areas (English language arts, mathematics, science, and social studies; Simms, 2016) based on state and national standards documents from across the United States. For example, the following are the measurement topics for grade 2 science (Simms, 2016).

- Object Composition
- Properties of Materials
- Changes to Materials
- Geographic Features
- Weathering and Erosion
- Earth's History
- Organism Needs
- Biodiversity

For each measurement topic, the team from Marzano Resources developed a proficiency scale. These scales are not intended for use as is; instead, a teacher or team of teachers should customize the scales, and specifically the score 2.0 content on the scale. The scales were intentionally designed with many targets at this level (more than can be optimally useful) so that teachers can select the ones that best fit their needs. In order to customize these scales, teacher teams should consider four options for each available score 2.0 learning target.

1. Leave the target exactly as is.
2. Delete the target.
3. Revise the target or add a replacement target.
4. Combine the target with another.

To illustrate, figure 2.5 and figure 2.6 (page 26) present the original and customized versions of the grade 2 scale Properties of Materials. While using the Critical Concepts scales still requires work, the time teachers need for scale development generally decreases significantly.

Guidance for Unique Situations

Proficiency scales can be developed for any content area. However, there are certain situations that seem to make the task of writing a proficiency scale more challenging than usual. When unique situations arise, it is helpful to remember the requirements for all proficiency scales.

1. A proficiency scale communicates priority content, which means that the content is explicitly taught and assessed.
2. A proficiency scale articulates a learning progression related to a priority standard or topic.
3. A proficiency scale allows students to reflect on their learning and track their progress.

While there are certain things that are true about all proficiency scales, these guidelines also affirm the fact that there is flexibility regarding scale development as well. Remembering this fact often eases the mind of scale developers when unique situations occur. In the following sections, we discuss guidance for standards that are too broad and for scales for young learners.

Properties of Materials (2 Science)	
4.0	The student will: • Test the effectiveness of different designs made of different materials that work for the same intended purpose (for example, determine the properties necessary for an effective oven mitt, identify different materials and designs for oven mitts as well as their properties, and determine which designs and materials are most effective by prioritizing which properties are most important)
3.5	In addition to score 3.0 performance, partial success at score 4.0 content
3.0	The student will: **PM1—Classify materials based on their observable properties** (for example, given a range of different materials, identify each material's various observable properties, and sort them into smaller groups based on these properties) **PM2—Determine which materials are best suited for an intended purpose based on their properties** (for example, given a specific purpose [such as an insulated mug or a warm glove], identify different types of materials that may be well suited for the purpose, test and compare their specific properties, and determine which would be most effective)
2.5	No major errors or omissions regarding score 2.0 content, and partial success at score 3.0 content
2.0	**PM1—**The student will recognize or recall specific vocabulary (for example, *absorbency, appearance, bent, ceramic, classify, color, cool, cut, drop, feel, flexibility, gas, group, hardness, heat, hit, liquid, material, matter, metal, observable, plastic, property, range, shininess, soak, solid, squeeze, state, strength, test, texture, wood*) and perform basic processes, such as: • Describe the three states of matter (solid, liquid, gas) • Describe different types of materials (for example, metals, plastics, wood, ceramic) • Explain that all materials have different properties • Explain a property as the way a material looks, feels, or behaves when it is heated, cooled, soaked, bent, cut, squeezed, hit, or dropped • List different properties (for example, those related to color, texture, hardness, flexibility, strength, absorbency, or shininess) • Identify a property of a material by looking at it • Identify a property of a material by testing it (for example, heating it up or bending it) **PM2—**The student will recognize or recall specific vocabulary (for example, *absorbency, appearance, bent, ceramic, color, compare, cool, cut, drop, effective, feel, flexibility, gas, hardness, heat, hit, liquid, material, matter, metal, observation, plastic, property, purpose, shininess, soak, solid, squeeze, state, strength, test, texture, wood*) and perform basic processes, such as: • Describe different types of materials (for example, metals, plastics, wood, ceramic) • Explain that all materials have different properties • Explain a property as the way a material looks, feels, or behaves when it is heated, cooled, soaked, bent, cut, squeezed, hit, or dropped • Identify the properties of a material through observation or testing • Identify properties necessary for a material to be suited for an intended purpose (for example, consider the properties necessary in a spoon that will be used to stir hot liquids)
1.5	Partial success at score 2.0 content, and major errors or omissions regarding score 3.0 content
1.0	With help, partial success at score 2.0 content and score 3.0 content
0.5	With help, partial success at score 2.0 content but not at score 3.0 content
0.0	Even with help, no success

Source: Adapted from Simms, 2016.

Figure 2.5: Original Critical Concepts scale.

Properties of Materials (2 Science)	
4.0	The student will: • Test the effectiveness of different designs made of different materials that work for the same intended purpose (for example, determine the properties necessary for an effective oven mitt, identify different materials and designs for oven mitts as well as their properties, and determine which designs and materials are most effective by prioritizing which properties are most important)
3.5	In addition to score 3.0 performance, partial success at score 4.0 content
3.0	The student will: **PM1—Classify materials based on their observable properties** (for example, given a range of different materials, identify each material's various observable properties, and sort them into smaller groups based on these properties) **PM2—Determine which materials are best suited for an intended purpose based on their properties** (for example, given a specific purpose [such as an insulated mug or a warm glove], identify different types of materials that may be well suited for the purpose, test and compare their specific properties, and determine which would be most effective)
2.5	No major errors or omissions regarding score 2.0 content, and partial success at score 3.0 content
2.0	**PM1—**The student will recognize or recall specific vocabulary (for example, *classify*, *matter*, *observable*, *property*, *state*) and perform basic processes, such as: • Describe the three states of matter (solid, liquid, gas) • Explain that all materials have different properties • List different properties (for example, those related to color, texture, hardness, flexibility, strength, absorbency, or shininess) • Identify a property of a material by observation and testing it (for example, heating it up or bending it) **PM2—**The student will recognize or recall specific vocabulary (for example, *compare*, *observation*, *test*) and perform basic processes, such as: • Describe different types of materials (for example, metals, plastics, wood, ceramic) • Explain a property as the way a material looks, feels, or behaves when it is heated, cooled, soaked, bent, cut, squeezed, hit, or dropped • Identify properties necessary for a material to be suited for an intended purpose (for example, consider the properties necessary in a spoon that will be used to stir hot liquids)
1.5	Partial success at score 2.0 content, and major errors or omissions regarding score 3.0 content
1.0	With help, partial success at score 2.0 content and score 3.0 content
0.5	With help, partial success at score 2.0 content but not at score 3.0 content
0.0	Even with help, no success

Source: Adapted from Simms, 2016.

Figure 2.6: Customized Critical Concepts scale.

Standards That Are Too Broad

In some cases, the standards for certain content areas or topics are very comprehensive and general in nature. While this can happen in any content area, this situation tends to relate most often to electives, such as fine arts and physical education. Consider this standard from one state for fine arts: "Students will use the creative process to make works of art exploring subjects and themes with a variety of materials" (FA 5.2.1, Nebraska Department of Education, 2014). How does a teacher or a team of teachers develop a scale when the standard is this broad? Some art teachers would even say that this standard includes almost anything they do in their classrooms! As a result of this vagueness, writing a high-quality scale may seem almost impossible. Because this standard is so general, teachers should determine more specific learning targets for the standard at a particular grade level *prior* to writing a proficiency scale. The following specific learning targets serve as examples of what a team of seventh-grade teachers might determine for this standard.

- The student will:
  - Compose a series of ideas to create original works of art
  - Compose with the elements of art and principles of design to communicate ideas into an original work of art
  - Prepare and exhibit their artwork

Once the team has identified these learning targets, writing a proficiency scale seems much easier to do. In fact, by determining the specific learning targets related to the broad standard, the team has created the score 3.0 content on the scale. Now they can simply follow one of the methods for developing a scale described previously in this chapter (page 17). Perhaps a team of art teachers decides that the second method, using a five-step process to determine score levels, would be the best method for developing a scale for this set of targets. Figure 2.7 shows an example of a seventh-grade art scale that teachers might have developed based on these learning targets.

Topic: Art

Grade Level or Course: Seventh grade

Standard: Students will use the creative process to make works of art exploring subjects and themes with a variety of materials.

Score 4.0: Complex Content

Demonstrations of learning that go above and beyond what was explicitly taught

The student will (for example):

- Analyze the use of the elements and principles of design in their artwork and the artwork of others

---

Score 3.0: Target Content

The expectations for all students

The student will:

- Compose with the elements of art and principles of design to communicate ideas into an original work of art
- Prepare and exhibit their artwork

Score 2.0: Simple Content

Foundational knowledge, simpler procedures, isolated details, vocabulary

The student will recognize or recall specific vocabulary, such as:

- *brainstorming list, cliché, symbol, media/medium, mind-mapping, plagiarism, thumbnail sketch*

The student will perform basic processes, such as:

- Compose a series of ideas to create original works of art (for example, three different sketches for one idea, evolving sketches for one idea, or multiple separate sketches for multiple separate ideas)
- Demonstrate knowledge of various elements of art and principles of design

---

Score 1.0: With help, the student can perform score 2.0 and 3.0 expectations.

Score 0.0: Even with help, the student cannot perform expectations.

Source: © 2019 by Columbus Public Schools. Used with permission.

Figure 2.7: Sample proficiency scale for art, grade 7.

In summary, when the standard is comprehensive and general in nature, it is often helpful for scale developers to determine the more specific learning targets related to the standard for a grade level or course prior to attempting to write a proficiency scale.

Scales for Young Learners

Standards for early elementary learners often include a phrase such as "with prompting and support." This is intended to indicate that a learner may not be developmentally ready to demonstrate the knowledge or skill independently, but when the teacher provides guidance and support, the student is able to perform the requirements. Consider the following Common Core reading standard for kindergarten: "With prompting and support, identify characters, settings, and major events in a story" (NGA & CCSSO, 2010a, RL.K.3). While it is appropriate because of the age of the learner to initiate the standard with the qualifying phrase, it creates challenges for scale users. For example, a kindergarten teacher must determine what constitutes "prompting and support" and how much to provide. The challenge increases when multiple teachers in the same school or district are making decisions about performance on this standard.

How can consistent decision making about mastery occur when it is likely that different teachers have different interpretations of this phrase?

One option for a teacher or teams to consider for overcoming this challenge is to identify, specifically, what constitutes prompting and support. In reference to the reading standard previously mentioned, teachers might agree on the following prompts and support.

- Define terms such as *character* and *setting* within the phrasing of a question (for example, Who were the characters in the story or who was the story mostly about?).

- Provide clues or hints (for example, "Think about the very beginning of the story").

- Use pictures within the story when asking questions (for example, pointing to a picture that will help a student answer a question).

While this option can be helpful, it may be easier to simply eliminate the phrase from the standard when developing a proficiency scale. While this increases the level of independence required of learners, it also eliminates the need to define prompting and support. Figure 2.8 exemplifies this option.

Priority Standard: With prompting and support, the student will identify characters, settings, and major events in a story. (RL.K.3)	
Score 4.0	The student will: • Predict the outcome when a character, the setting, or a major event is changed
Score 3.0	The student will: • Identify characters, settings, and major events in a grade-appropriate story
Score 2.0	The student will: • Understand key vocabulary, such as: *character*, *event*, *setting*, *story* • Recognize characters, settings, and a major event in a grade-appropriate story

Source: Adapted from Marzano et al., 2013, p. 93.

Figure 2.8: Sample scale for reading, kindergarten.

Summary

This chapter communicates the idea that there are multiple ways to go about developing proficiency scales. Schools and districts may choose which method to use and may even approach scale development using a blend of the methods described.

In addition to methods for scale development, this chapter shared other important information pertinent to the scale development process: adapting existing scales and responding to unique situations. The next chapter will focus on score 4.0, the complex content on a proficiency scale.

Chapter 2 Comprehension Questions

1. What are some different methods for developing a proficiency scale? What are the advantages of each method? What might be a drawback of any method described?

2. What is true about every proficiency scale, regardless of the method chosen for development?

3. What is important to remember about writing a proficiency scale for a standard that is very broad and comprehensive?

4. What are two options for scales when a phrase such as "with prompting and support" is part of the standard? What are the positive aspects and challenges of each option?

CHAPTER 3

Score 4.0: Complex Content

Score 4.0 on a proficiency scale describes how a learner might demonstrate more than what the standard requires. While not all learners will attain this level, it is critical to give students who reach proficiency an opportunity to extend their learning. This includes students who enter a grade level or course having already mastered the grade-level standards, as well as students who tend to learn new content very quickly. In essence, the language at score 4.0 on a proficiency scale provides guidance to teachers about how to enrich learning opportunities for students who are able to apply their knowledge and skill.

As mentioned in chapter 1 (page 5), the statements recorded at score 4.0 on proficiency scales are examples of how students might apply or make inferences based on the target content. By definition, score 4.0 goes beyond the level of the standard, so there is no single expectation. A student can demonstrate a score 4.0 performance in numerous ways; hence, the words *for example* typically appear prior to the score 4.0 content.

In order to ensure quality score 4.0 content, there are a few specific guidelines for scale development teams or individual teachers to consider. These include the following.

1. **Increase cognitive difficulty:** The level of cognition that score 4.0 requires of learners

should go beyond the level of cognition required at score 3.0.

2. **Require application of knowledge and skill:** The score 4.0 targets should not be about quantity or quality of work; instead, learners should be required to demonstrate application of the knowledge and skills acquired at the lower levels of the scale.

3. **Avoid repurposing content from other scales:** The content at score 4.0 should not simply be the score 3.0 expectation in the following grade level or course.

The remainder of this chapter will provide information about each of these guidelines, as well as examples to ensure clear understanding of this important level of the proficiency scale. Appendix D (page 145) presents additional examples of score 4.0 content.

Increase Cognitive Difficulty

To understand how cognitive difficulty increases for score 4.0, it is helpful to revisit the generic form of the scale, as shown in figure 3.1 (page 32). As we examine these levels from score 0.0 upward, it is clear that the cognition required of a learner increases with each level until, at score 4.0, the learner must make inferences or demonstrate other higher-order thinking skills. The increasing cognitive challenge becomes even more obvious when we fill in academic content at levels 2.0 through 4.0, as in figure 3.2.

At score 2.0, the verbs *understand* and *identify* require simple recall of the learner. The level of cognition increases at score 3.0, as the learner is asked to *compare and contrast*, as well as *explain*. Finally, at score 4.0, the learner is required to *analyze*, which is the highest level of cognition represented on the scale. When a learning progression is well articulated, the thinking required of the student grows as he or she moves up on the scale.

While the example in figure 3.2 focuses on the verbs in each learning target, there are other ways to indicate a more sophisticated level of thinking at higher scale levels. For example, consider the following two learning targets from two different levels on the same proficiency scale.

1. **Score 2.0:** The student will identify a print resource (for example, book, magazine, newspaper).

2. **Score 3.0:** The student will identify fiction versus nonfiction text.

Though the verb is the same in these two statements, the score 3.0 target still requires a higher

Score 4.0	In addition to exhibiting level 3 performance, in-depth inferences and applications that go beyond what was taught in class
Score 3.0	No major errors or omissions regarding any of the information and processes (simple or complex) that were explicitly taught
Score 2.0	No major errors or omissions regarding the simpler details and processes, but major errors or omissions regarding the more complex ideas and processes
Score 1.0	With help, partial knowledge of some of the simpler and complex details and processes
Score 0.0	Even with help, no understanding or skill demonstrated

Source: Adapted from Marzano, 2010.

Figure 3.1: Generic form of a proficiency scale.

Priority Standard: The student will compare and contrast various forms of government and explain how governments determine citizen participation.	
Score 4.0	The student will: • Analyze how citizen participation within Latin American governments has changed over time, including modern-day events
Score 3.0	The student will: • Compare and contrast various forms of government • Explain how different governments determine citizen participation
Score 2.0	The student will: • Understand key vocabulary, such as *autocratic, oligarchic, democratic, parliamentary democracy, presidential democracy* • Identify different ways citizens can participate in governments

Source: © 2019 by Fulton County Schools. Used with permission.

Figure 3.2: A proficiency scale related to citizen participation in government.

level of cognition. The score 2.0 learning target requires simple recall. For score 3.0, the learner would need to know characteristics of both fiction and nonfiction text in order to demonstrate mastery of the target.

Taxonomies that define levels of cognitive demand can be extremely helpful in designing scales that appropriately increase the level of difficulty as learners move toward score 4.0. There are numerous taxonomies available. For one, Marzano and Kendall (2007) proposed *The New Taxonomy of Educational Objectives*. This taxonomy is made up of six levels of processing and three domains of knowledge. The first four levels of processing comprise the cognitive system and are thus quite helpful to scale developers as they articulate score 4.0 content. Table 3.1 displays the four levels of the cognitive system, mental processes within each level, and example verbs and phrases that often signify a specific mental process.

When using a taxonomy to write score 4.0 learning targets, teachers can follow two steps in order to increase the level of cognitive demand on the proficiency scale.

Table 3.1: The New Taxonomy of Educational Objectives—The Cognitive System

Level of Difficulty	Mental Process	Verbs and Phrases	
Level 4 **Knowledge Utilization**	Decision Making	Select the best among the following alternatives Which among the following would be the best?	What is the best way? Which of these is more suitable? Decide
	Problem Solving	Solve How would you overcome? Adapt Develop a strategy to	Figure out a way to How will you reach your goal under these conditions?
	Experimenting	Experiment Generate and test Test the idea that What would happen if? How would you test that?	How would you determine if? How can this be explained? Based on the experiment, what can be predicted?
	Investigating	Investigate Research Find out about Take a position on	What are the differing features of? How did this happen? Why did this happen? What would happen if?
Level 3 **Analysis**	Matching and Comparative Analysis	Categorize Compare and contrast Differentiate Discriminate	Distinguish Sort Create an analogy Create a metaphor
	Classifying	Classify Organize Sort	Identify a broader category Identify categories Identify different types

continued ⇨

Level 3 **Analysis**	Analyzing Errors	Identify errors Identify problems Identify issues Identify misunderstandings Assess	Critique Diagnose Evaluate Edit Revise
	Generalizing	Generalize What conclusions can be drawn? What inferences can be made? Create a generalization	Create a principle Create a rule Trace the development of Form conclusions
	Specifying	Make and defend Predict Judge Deduct	What would have to happen? Develop an argument for Under what conditions?
Level 2 **Comprehension**	Integrating	Describe how or why Describe the key parts Describe the effects Describe the relationship between	Explain ways in which Paraphrase Summarize
	Symbolizing	Symbolize Depict Represent Illustrate Draw	Show Use Model Diagram Chart
Level 1 **Retrieval**	Recognizing	Recognize (from a list) Select from (a list)	Identify (from a list) Determine if the following statements are true
	Recalling	Exemplify Name List Label State	Describe Identify who Describe what Identify when
	Executing	Use Demonstrate Show	Make Complete Draft

Source: Marzano & Kendall, 2007.

1. Determine the cognitive level of score 3.0 on the proficiency scale. If there are multiple targets, determine the level of each learning target and use the highest level as the starting point for increasing the level of cognitive demand.

2. Choose an appropriate verb from a level of the taxonomy that is higher than the level of score 3.0; write a score 4.0 target beginning with the chosen verb.

For the purpose of demonstrating how these two steps can be executed in relation to The New Taxonomy, consider the learning targets related to the nonacademic topic of staying focused in figure 3.3.

Score 2.0 contains the verb *recognize*, and score 3.0 contains *execute*. Both of these verbs appear within Level 1: Retrieval of The New Taxonomy. While in the same level of difficulty, *execute* requires a higher level of cognition than does *recognize*. In order to complete the progression of knowledge from score 2.0 to score 4.0, scale developers can consider a verb from a higher level in the taxonomy. For example, the score 4.0 content in figure 3.4 employs the verb *describe*, which is found in Level 2: Comprehension. It clearly requires a higher level of thinking than does *recognize* or *execute*, in the manner that these verbs are used on this particular proficiency scale.

As a second example, consider Bloom's Taxonomy Revised (Anderson & Krathwohl, 2001) and the action verbs associated with each level of the framework, as shown in table 3.2 (page 36). Consider the following score 3.0 learning target from a high school economics proficiency scale: "The student will explain the advantages and disadvantages of types of business ownership in our economy." The verb *explain* suggests that this learning target falls within Bloom's category of Understanding. In order to increase the cognitive demand, the teacher can select a verb from any category higher on the taxonomy than Understanding—Applying, Analyzing, Evaluating, or Creating. This process might result in the following score 4.0 learning target: "The student will critique a scenario to determine whether or not the type of business ownership has more advantages or disadvantages." The verb *critique* falls under Bloom's category of Evaluating, which suggests a significant increase in the cognitive demand expected of the learner.

This same process can occur with other frameworks as well, such as Norman Webb's Depth of Knowledge, which determines the level of rigor of a task (Miller, 2018). Figure 3.5 shows the four levels that make up the framework.

Score 3.0	The student will execute a simple teacher-provided strategy for staying focused when answers or solutions are not immediately apparent.
Score 2.0	The student will recognize when he or she is or is not staying focused when answers or solutions are not immediately apparent.

Source: Adapted from Simms, 2016.

Figure 3.3: Score 2.0 and score 3.0 content for staying focused.

Score 4.0	The student will describe possible effects of staying focused and not staying focused when answers or solutions are not immediately apparent.
Score 3.0	The student will execute a simple teacher-provided strategy for staying focused when answers or solutions are not immediately apparent.
Score 2.0	The student will recognize when he or she is or is not staying focused when answers or solutions are not immediately apparent.

Source: Adapted from Simms, 2016.

Figure 3.4: Complete scale for staying focused.

Level 1 Acquired Knowledge	Involves recall and reproduction. Remembering facts or defining a procedure.
Level 2 Knowledge Application	Skills and concepts. Students use learned concepts to answer questions.
Level 3 Analysis	Involves strategic thinking. Complexity increases here and involves planning, justification, and complex reasoning. Explains how concepts and procedures can be used to provide results.
Level 4 Augmentation	Extended thinking. This requires going beyond the standard learning and asking, How else can the learning be used in real-world contexts?

Source: Miller, 2018.

Figure 3.5: Webb's Depth of Knowledge framework.

Table 3.2: Action Verbs for Bloom's Taxonomy Revised

Remembering	Understanding	Applying	Analyzing	Evaluating	Creating
Choose	Classify	Apply	Analyze	Agree	Adapt
Define	Compare	Build	Assume	Appraise	Build
Find	Contrast	Choose	Categorize	Assess	Change
How	Demonstrate	Construct	Classify	Award	Choose
Label	Explain	Develop	Compare	Choose	Combine
List	Extend	Experiment	Conclusion	Compare	Compile
Match	Illustrate	Identify	Contrast	Conclude	Compose
Name	Infer	Interview	Discover	Criteria	Construct
Omit	Interpret	Make use of	Dissect	Criticize	Create
Recall	Outline	Model	Distinguish	Critique	Delete
Relate	Relate	Organize	Divide	Decide	Design
Select	Rephrase	Plan	Examine	Deduct	Develop
Show	Show	Select	Function	Defend	Discuss
Spell	Summarize	Solve	Inference	Determine	Elaborate
Tell	Translate	Utilize	Inspect	Disprove	Estimate
What			List	Estimate	Formulate
When			Motive	Evaluate	Imagine
Where			Relationships	Explain	Improve
Which			Simplify	Importance	Invent
Who			Survey	Influence	Make up
Why			Take part in	Interpret	Maximize
			Text for	Judge	Minimize
			Theme	Justify	Modify
				Mark	Originate
				Measure	Plan
				Opinion	Predict
				Perceive	Propose
				Prioritize	Solve
				Prove	Suggest
				Rate	Test
				Recommend	Theory
				Select	
				Support	
				Value	

The four descriptions in figure 3.5 provide conceptual understanding, but for writing a score 4.0 learning target, Webb's verb wheel may be more helpful (see figure 3.6). A teacher can simply follow the same two steps of determining the cognitive level of the score 3.0 content and selecting a verb from a higher level as the basis for score 4.0.

Require Application of Knowledge and Skill

In order to be certain that application of knowledge and skill is required of learners, a score 4.0 learning target should require the integration of score 3.0 learning targets. Stated differently, a task

Depth of Knowledge (DOK) Levels

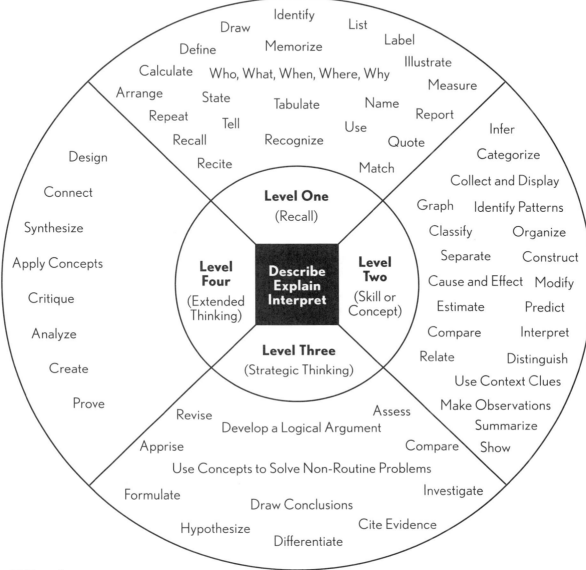

Source: Webb et al., 2005.

Figure 3.6: Webb's verb wheel.

that requires application of knowledge and skill combines all score 3.0 learning targets into a single score 4.0 learning target. Consider the score 3.0 and score 4.0 grade 5 ELA learning targets for analyzing claims, evidence, and reasoning in figure 3.7.

To evaluate a score 4.0 descriptor, then, a teacher or team of teachers can ask, Does the score 4.0 learning target require mastery of all score 3.0 learning targets? In figure 3.7, a student could not be successful on the score 4.0 target if he or she

Score 4.0	Evaluate the argument in a text and decide whether or not the author has sufficiently defended his or her claims.
Score 3.0	• Delineate a text's argument and its specific claims. • Distinguish claims that are supported by evidence and reasoning from claims that are not.

Source: Adapted from Simms, 2016.

Figure 3.7: A score 4.0 learning target that integrates two score 3.0 targets.

was not able to demonstrate both score 3.0 learning targets.

A common pitfall when developing score 4.0 content is to write a learning goal that references the quality or quantity of work completed, rather than requiring application. Scale development teams must stay away from this ineffective shortcut when crafting score 4.0 language. For example, a high school career and technical education proficiency scale for welding includes the following learning target at score 3.0: "The learner will use identified safety practices when utilizing shop technology to complete assigned tasks and projects" (Wyoming State Board of Education, 2014, CV12.2.4). Now consider the following three examples of potential score 4.0 language.

1. The learner will always use identified safety practices when utilizing shop technology to complete assigned tasks and projects.

2. The learner will explain why identified safety practices are required, including examples of potential outcomes of unsafe practice.

3. The learner will self-correct when exercising unsafe practices in the shop and explain why the practice was unsafe.

The first example is the same as the score 3.0 learning target, with the addition of the word *always*. The inclusion of this one word doesn't raise the cognitive difficulty or require the student to demonstrate application of knowledge or skill. In fact, the score 3.0 learning target already requires consistent use of safe practices; "the learner will use identified safety practices" implies that it occurs most or all of the time. The score 3.0 learning target is also more realistic, as *always* does not allow any room for occasional student error.

The second and third options are better score 4.0 learning targets, as they do require the learner to go beyond the score 3.0 learning target. The second option requires the learner to not only use safe practices, but to be able to generate potential outcomes should safe practices not be exercised. The third option requires the skill of self-monitoring when practice is unsafe. Both clearly require more than the score 3.0 learning target. In general, words that reference quantity or quality are reserved for rubrics (see chapter 5, page 59), not proficiency scales.

The following vignette showcases a teacher developing a score 4.0 learning target that requires knowledge application.

Dan DeMuth teaches seventh-grade science and has worked with his collaborative team to determine score 2.0 and score 3.0 learning targets for their proficiency scales. His team has decided to divide and conquer the score 4.0 learning targets, so each team member has three or four scales to address. Dan is currently working on the scale about inheriting traits. On this particular scale, the score 3.0 content requires students to:

- Construct an explanation, supported by scientific evidence, of the role of genes and chromosomes in the process of inheriting a specific trait
- Construct and solve a Punnett square using vocabulary clues (for example, *heterozygous, homozygous, dominant, recessive*)

It is time for Dan to go about the business of developing score 4.0 learning targets. He wants to be sure to increase the level of thinking required of students and include an element of application, so he chooses the verb *investigate* to be the beginning word of his score 4.0 learning target. He also includes an element of explanation within the target, therefore requiring two different thought processes of students. His final score 4.0 target asks students to:

- Investigate various genetic disorders or mutations associated with genes and chromosomes in the process of inheriting a specific trait and explain the disorder or

> mutation and its effect on cells, tissues, and organs
>
> He is confident that the level of thinking required in this score 4.0 learning target is greater than the thinking required in either of the score 3.0 learning targets. It also requires that students master and apply both score 3.0 targets in order to be successful with the more advanced task. Dan will take his score 4.0 work back to his collaborative team the next time they meet for feedback and revision.

Source for learning targets: © 2019 by Fulton County Schools. Used with permission.

Avoid Repurposing Content From Other Scales

When creating score 4.0 content, avoid repurposing the requirements of the next grade level or course—for example, using a sixth-grade 3.0 target as a fifth-grade 4.0 target. While one might intuitively think that this approach makes sense, this is not the preferred means of determining the content at this level. Score 4.0 must require a more complex performance of the target content, or application of the knowledge and skill acquired by mastering score 3.0. Consider the following two elementary mathematics standards.

- **Grade 1:** The learner will tell and write time in hours and half-hours using analog and digital clocks.

- **Grade 2:** The learner will tell and write time from analog and digital clocks to the nearest five minutes, using a.m. and p.m.

Because of the relationship of these two standards, teacher teams may be inclined to use the second-grade standard as the score 4.0 content on this first-grade proficiency scale. After all, it does require more of learners than does the grade 1 standard. However, it is simply a more detailed version of the content; it does not increase the cognitive

difficulty or require the application of the 3.0 content.

The grade 1 proficiency scale in figure 3.8 presents a better example of a score 4.0 performance. The learning target presented at score 4.0 requires the learner to *apply* the understanding acquired through mastery of score 3.0. It is not the second-grade standard; instead, it increases the challenge and complexity of the grade 1 standard. This is good practice, as it allows students to learn the content in the following grade level during the appropriate academic year.

MEASUREMENT, DATA, STATISTICS, AND PROBABILITY Time: Grade 1	
Score 4.0	The student will (for example): • Advance a given time by a specified number of hours or half-hours
Score 3.0	The student will: • Tell and write time in hours and half-hours using analog and digital clocks
Score 2.0	The student will: • Understand key vocabulary, such as *analog, digital, hour, half-hour* • Identify the hands on an analog clock • Identify time written in the correct format

Source: © 2019 by Fulton County Schools. Used with permission.

Figure 3.8: Proficiency scale for time, grade 1.

Summary

This chapter has described three guidelines for writing high-quality score 4.0 learning targets. First, score 4.0 should require a higher level of cognition than that which is required at score 3.0 on the scale. This can be accomplished in several ways, but a taxonomy or framework for levels of thinking can be helpful. The second guideline reminds scale developers that score 4.0 learning targets should require a student to apply their understanding of the target content (score 3.0). The final guideline suggests that the next grade level or course can inform the development of a score 4.0 learning target, but it should not typically *become* the score 4.0 learning target. Based on the guidelines presented in this chapter, teachers and scale developers can identify complex content for every grade level and any course. Having covered the development of proficiency scales, the next chapter will begin our exploration of their use in schools.

Chapter 3 Comprehension Questions

1. Why is score 4.0 included on a proficiency scale?

2. What is important to remember about the cognition required of students in relation to score 4.0 on a proficiency scale? How can scale development teams ensure these things are true?

3. Why is score 4.0 typically not the expectation articulated in the next grade level or course?

CHAPTER 4
The Use of Proficiency Scales in the Classroom

Once an individual teacher, a teacher team, a school, or a district has taken the time to develop proficiency scales, these valuable tools can and should be used daily in the classroom. While the scale *development* process primarily involves teachers, the *use* of scales goes well beyond that group. If we are to achieve the full impact of proficiency scales in supporting the learning process, teachers, students, and parents must all utilize the scales.

Teacher Use of Proficiency Scales

Four critical components of effective pedagogy are curriculum, instruction, assessment, and feedback. In a classroom where proficiency scales exist, all four of these components are based on the scales. To illustrate, consider a grade 2 ELA unit of instruction on informational texts that includes three priority reading standards. These three standards are the primary focus of a teacher's planning process. They also serve as the basis for the teacher's determination of which strategies to use as he or she teaches the content on each scale. The scales serve as the foundation for the assessment processes that occur over the course of this unit, and ultimately, they provide a means for offering students feedback on their current levels of performance on each of the scales. Figure 4.1 shows

these four components of pedagogy in relation to proficiency scales. As the image suggests, scales are the center of effective classroom pedagogy. For the purpose of the discussion in this chapter, consider the second-grade ELA proficiency scale in figure 4.2 (page 44).

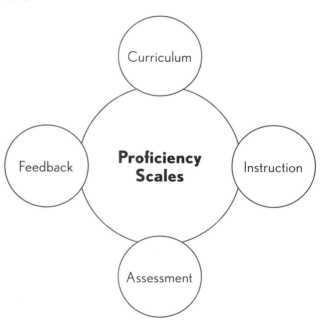

Source: Adapted from Heflebower et al., 2019.

Figure 4.1: The role of proficiency scales.

Curriculum

The first use of scales by a classroom teacher relates to curriculum. Suppose that the text features scale in figure 4.2 is one of numerous second-grade proficiency scales that make up the curriculum for English language arts. A manageable set of twelve to fifteen proficiency scales for each grade level and subject area defines a curriculum that is both guaranteed and viable—*guaranteed* in that it is consistent across classrooms and *viable* in that there is enough instructional time to address all the content (Marzano, Warrick, & Simms, 2014). Regarding the importance of a guaranteed and viable curriculum, Marzano (2003) stated:

> I rank this as the first factor having the most impact on student achievement. A guaranteed and viable curriculum is primarily a combination of my factors "opportunity to learn" and "time." Both have strong correlations with academic achievement, yet they are so interdependent that they constitute one factor. (p. 22)

In essence, each proficiency scale represents a non-negotiable topic that all students must know or be able to do by the end of the school year or course. As a result, a teacher will work diligently to ensure adequate instructional time is spent on each of the scales that make up the curriculum. Additionally, he or she will ensure adequate instructional resources are available for teaching the content on the scales. If a textbook is one of the instructional resources, a teacher will likely identify the parts that support teaching any target on a scale. Finally, a teacher will

ENGLISH LANGUAGE ARTS	
Grade 2 Text Features	
Score 4.0	In addition to score 3.0 performance, the student demonstrates in-depth inferences and applications that go beyond what was taught. The student will: • Make a suggestion for an additional text feature to a grade-appropriate text and provide a rationale for this decision
Score 3.5	In addition to score 3.0 performance, partial success at score 4.0 content
Score 3.0	The student will: • Use text features to locate information and gain meaning from print and digital grade-level text (Guided Reading Level M)
Score 2.5	No major errors or omissions regarding score 2.0 content, and partial success at score 3.0 content
Score 2.0	The student will recognize or recall specific vocabulary, such as: *context clues, infer, text features.* There are no major errors or omissions regarding the simpler details and processes as the student: • Identifies text features (for example, illustration, diagram, glossary, headings, bold print, captions, graphs) However, the student exhibits major errors or omissions regarding the more complex ideas and processes.
Score 1.5	Partial success at score 2.0 content, and major errors or omissions regarding score 3.0 content
Score 1.0	With help, partial success at score 2.0 content and score 3.0 content
Score 0.5	With help, partial success at score 2.0 content but not at score 3.0 content

Source: © 2016 by South Sioux City Community Schools. Used with permission.

Figure 4.2: Proficiency scale for text features, grade 2.

consider how he or she will monitor progress toward the goals on each scale. All of this happens in an effort to exercise the idea that scales are the guaranteed and viable curriculum.

Because of the importance of the content on a proficiency scale, the proficiency scale itself should be part of the curriculum. Teachers typically spend some time ensuring all students understand what proficiency scales are, why they are important, and how they will be used in the classroom. This explicit instruction regarding proficiency scales usually occurs early in an academic school year, sometimes even during the first few days that students are in the classroom. Of course, the instruction about proficiency scales looks different based on the age of the learners and the personal instructional style of the teacher. The amount of time spent varies depending on whether or not students have encountered proficiency scales in previous grade levels or courses. Regardless, teachers who seek to increase student achievement through the use of proficiency scales must make sure students have a solid understanding of proficiency scales.

We will further discuss using pacing guides to plan curriculum around proficiency scales in chapter 5 (page 70).

Instruction

The second use of scales by classroom teachers relates to planning and delivering instruction. The following quote is from third-grade teacher Kylie Johanson, who uses scales in the classroom on a daily basis:

> Pretty much everything I do planning-wise relates to content on proficiency scales. I hold myself accountable to providing direct instruction to the content at scores 2.0 and 3.0 on my scales for my third graders.

> Sometimes the attention I need to give the score 2.0 content on my current scale is minimal, as students come to me already having some understanding of these targets. Sometimes I have to spend more time there to ensure they all attain mastery of the score 3.0 target or targets. I use my proficiency scales as my instructional planning guide. (personal communication, April 17, 2019)

Since the scale articulates a learning progression, it makes intuitive sense that in most cases the score 2.0 content will be taught prior to addressing the learning targets at score 3.0 on the scale.

Some teachers begin the majority of lessons by communicating the scale level being addressed that day. In reference to the proficiency scale for text features (figure 4.2), a teacher might begin his or her lesson by stating the following.

> *We are continuing to learn about text features, boys and girls, as part of our unit on informational texts. Today, we will begin with a review of the vocabulary at score 2.0 on our scale. Then we will work on the other score 2.0 learning target. We are going to be talking a lot today about illustrations, which is one of the text features all second graders need to know about.*

By introducing the lesson with the proficiency scale, the teacher is effectively communicating to students what they need to know and be able to do.

One facet of instructional planning is determining appropriate activities and assignments for learners. When proficiency scales are the basis for instructional planning, each activity should connect to learning targets on the scale. Figure 4.3 (page 46) displays sample instructional activities for each level of the grade 2 proficiency scale for text features.

Grade 2 Text Features		
	Learning Targets	**Sample Activities**
Score 4.0	In addition to score 3.0 performance, the student demonstrates in-depth inferences and applications that go beyond what was taught. The student will: • Make a suggestion for an additional text feature to a grade-appropriate text and provide a rationale for this decision	• Explain why or why not a text feature is helpful to the reader. • Suggest additional text features to a piece of informational text.
Score 3.0	The student will: • Use text features to locate information and gain meaning from print and digital grade-level text (Guided Reading Level M)	• Given an unknown word, students will be able to use text features to infer or gain meaning of the unknown word. For example, "Plumage is the feathers on a bird. I used the glossary and the diagram and labels on page 32."
Score 2.0	The student will recognize or recall specific vocabulary, such as: *context clues*, *infer*, *text features*. There are no major errors or omissions regarding the simpler details and processes as the student: • Identifies text features (for example, illustration, diagram, glossary, headings, bold print, captions, graphs) However, the student exhibits major errors or omissions regarding the more complex ideas and processes.	• Given a text feature sample, students will correctly identify it. Example: Give students a diagram of a bird. Students will identify a picture as a diagram with labels. Example: When given a reading passage with an unknown word, students re-read the sentence to attempt to identify meaning.

Source: © 2016 by South Sioux City Community Schools. Used with permission.

Figure 4.3: Sample activities for a text features proficiency scale.

The following vignette features a second-grade teacher who has planned a classroom activity related to score 2.0 on the scale.

Miss Jones recently began teaching the content that is on her second-grade ELA proficiency scale about text features. She knows that if her students are to be successful in using the text features to locate specific information in nonfiction texts, they need to know about a defined set of text features, such as illustrations, diagrams, and graphs. On the previous day of instruction, Miss Jones explicitly taught her students about the various text features. She showed the students different examples of text features in nonfiction texts that they had studied earlier in the year.

She begins today's lesson by asking students to review the different text features with a discussion partner. The review activity asks students to match a text feature with its description. The information appears on notecards, making it easy for students to position the text feature next to its description. When each pair finishes, Miss Jones meets with the students to answer any questions they have or correct any wrong matches. Once this partner activity is complete, she hands out a single-sided practice sheet for students to complete independently. At the end of the lesson, Miss Jones asks students to reflect on their understanding of the content at score 2.0 on the proficiency scale. Before students leave the room for recess, she asks them to record their current scale score on a sticky note, stating why they assigned themselves that particular score. Students place their sticky notes on the door as they leave the classroom.

When teachers use the proficiency scale to plan instruction, students see the connection between activities or assignments and the scale. This positive instructional practice ensures that all students understand the value of the classroom activities and assignments. Additionally, when a teacher knows precisely what knowledge and skill students need to learn, instruction becomes more focused, optimizing the use of instructional time.

In order to ensure that each proficiency scale within a grade level or course receives adequate instructional focus, it is beneficial for a teacher or team of teachers to engage in developing units of instruction. Marzano addressed this idea in *The New Art and Science of Teaching* (2017) when he stated, "I believe it is an ineffective practice to plan one lesson at a time. Instead, teachers should plan from the perspective of the unit, which should provide an overarching framework for instruction" (p. 107).

When making decisions about instructional units, it works well for a team of teachers to consider all of the available proficiency scales and to make decisions about which scales make logical sense to teach within the same unit. For example, in the previously mentioned example unit of instruction on informational text, the grade 2 team includes the following three scales: text features, central idea, and connections. The decision to include these three scales in the unit was based on the fact that all three scales are about informational text. The team determines numerous other instructional units as well, perhaps a total of five to seven instructional units for the entire academic year. It is important to note that some scales may

be included in more than one instructional unit to ensure adequate instructional focus and to increase the likelihood that students will master the content by the end of the year or course.

Figure 4.4 displays the instructional units identified by the grade 2 team and the reading proficiency scales (indicated by standards) included within each unit, as well as the approximate duration of time to be spent teaching each unit. As you can see, most of the proficiency scales are part of more than one instructional unit.

Unit 1 (six weeks) Characters	Unit 2 (six weeks) Literary Text	Unit 3 (four weeks) Informational Text
RL 2, 3, 4, 5 RI 2	RL 2, 3, 4, 5	RI 2, 3, 5
Unit 4 (four weeks) Author's Purpose and Point of View	Unit 5 (seven weeks) How Meaning Is Developed	Unit 6 (six weeks) Putting It All Together
RL 6 RI 6, 8	RL 2, 3, 4, 5	RI 2, 6, 9

Figure 4.4: Sample unit plan.

After determining units of instruction, a teacher or team of teachers can go about the business of planning daily instruction. As this planning occurs, teachers make decisions about which strategies and resources to use to deliver content to learners. Teachers will also decide on the best activities to include within a single lesson and ultimately about work to assign in relation to the content. Finally, daily planning includes how to monitor progress toward any target on a proficiency scale included in the unit of instruction.

Assessment

At any point in time during instruction, the classroom teacher may decide that he or she needs to assess students' understanding. Assessment is anything a teacher does to gather information about what a student knows or is able to do related to a specific topic—not just traditional tests. In *The New Art and Science of Teaching*, Marzano (2017) discussed formal and informal assessment:

> At its core, assessment is a feedback mechanism for students and teachers. Assessments should provide students with information about how to advance their understanding of content and teachers with information about how to help students do so. The desired mental states and processes for assessment are that: Students understand how test scores and grades relate to their status on the progression of knowledge they are expected to master. To achieve these outcomes in students, there must be a transparent relationship between students' scores on assessments and their progress on a proficiency scale. (p. 21)

Informal assessment will occur more frequently than formal assessment—typically daily. This type of assessment doesn't feel test-like to a learner. In fact, students may not even be aware that they are being assessed when this type of assessment is used by a teacher. A few informal assessment ideas a teacher may implement in relation to the proficiency scale for text features include: (1) probing conversations with students to determine whether they can identify the various text features listed on the scale; (2) providing students with individual note cards that list a single text feature to hold up in association with a teacher-provided description of a text feature; and (3) a matching activity that students complete at the end of a class period.

There will be times, though, when a teacher determines that formal assessment—such as a test, project, or presentation—is appropriate. When this is the case, the teacher must ensure that items and tasks align to the language on the proficiency scale. Figure 4.5 displays assessment items that align with language on the proficiency scale for text features. The example score 2.0 item requires simple recall on the part of the learner, which is often the case with items at this level. Common score 2.0 item types are multiple choice, true or false, matching, and fill in the blank. In most cases, these item types are very appropriate because of the fact that score 2.0 is simple content.

The example score 3.0 item in figure 4.5 requires a higher level of thinking than does the score 2.0 item.

Score 4.0	Make a suggestion for an additional text feature to a grade-appropriate text and provide a rationale for this decision.	What additional text feature would you add to the passage "All About Martin Luther King"? Why would you add this text feature?
Score 3.0	Use text features to locate information and gain meaning from print and digital grade-level text.	Explain why the caption under the picture is important for a reader. *A scientist from the Environmental Protection Agency tests water quality after an oil spill.*
Score 2.0	Identify text features (for example, illustration, diagram, glossary, headings, bold print, captions, graphs).	Write the name of the text feature.

Source: © 2016 by South Sioux City Community Schools. Used with permission.

Figure 4.5: Sample assessment items for a text features proficiency scale.

Some common score 3.0 item types include short constructed response, extended response, and performance tasks. Finally, the example score 4.0 item requires the learner to apply his or her knowledge. Notice what the complex content learning target requires—the student must provide a rationale for a decision he or she made. In many cases, score 4.0 items require a learner to exercise decision making, problem solving, investigation, or experimentation. Clearly, these processes demand that a learner have strong command of the score 3.0 content in order to be successful on the score 4.0 assessment task. Appendix E (page 147) contains additional examples of scales and related assessment items.

Given that both informal and formal assessments will be administered periodically during a unit of instruction, it is important to discuss the number of assessments that should contribute to a teacher's decision about a student's current level of performance on a scale. Marzano (2006) recommended four or five assessments per topic during a grading period. Having said this, it is important to remember that these scores may be a combination of formal and informal assessment.

Feedback

When informal and formal assessments are based on a proficiency scale, it becomes easier for a teacher to offer students meaningful feedback. As we did in chapter 1 (page 14), let's assume that most educators agree that effective feedback is timely, specific, and corrective. That means that a teacher should offer feedback to a learner soon after the assessment opportunity. It also means that the feedback gives the student clear direction on how to improve. In some instances, the feedback is also a celebration of student learning.

Suppose that one second-grade student earns the assessment scores in figure 4.6 for the text features

proficiency scale (figure 4.2, page 44). It would make sense for the teacher, at any point in time, to have a conversation with the student that sounds like the following.

You are making great progress on our scale for text features. It appears that you know the score 2.0 content and that you also have strong understanding of the score 3.0 learning targets. Awesome job! I'll bet that if you keep working hard, you may even have success on the score 4.0 target at some point in the near future!

This feedback gives the student a good idea of where he or she is on the learning progression.

There will also likely be times when a teacher provides a learner more specific feedback about his or her performance on a particular learning target on the scale. A conversation with a student who has mastered the score 2.0 content but is still working on score 3.0 may sound like the following.

It's clear that you really know the different text features that we have learned about, like diagrams and headings. That's awesome because you need to be able to identify them in order to use those text features! Since you can identify text features, now let's work on using them to better understand what you read. Let's focus on what information you can learn from each type of text feature.

Feedback of this nature helps a learner know where he or she needs to exert effort in order to move up the proficiency scale. It also shows the learner that he or she has acquired some knowledge or skill already, which often results in motivation to learn even more.

When proficiency scales are the basis for curriculum, instruction, assessment, and feedback, the teacher is able to provide focused lessons that result in clarity among students about what they need to know and be able to do.

Text Features	Score 1 (informal)	Score 2 (informal)	Score 3 (formal)	Score 4 (informal)	Score 5 (formal)
	2.0	2.0	2.5	3.0	3.0

Figure 4.6: Sample proficiency scale scores.

Student Use of Proficiency Scales

There are numerous ways that students can benefit from using proficiency scales in the classroom. In *The New Art and Science of Teaching*, Marzano (2017) presented a design question for teachers to ask themselves: "How will I communicate clear learning goals that help students understand the progression of knowledge they are expected to master and where they are along that progression?" (p. 6). The implication of this question is, of course, that students have solid understanding of what proficiency scales are, why they are important, and how they will be used in the classroom. Another implication of this question is that, at any point in time, a student should know where he or she stands in relation to the content on a proficiency scale. In service of these goals, a teacher may engage students in using the proficiency scales in three ways: (1) reflecting on their current level of performance through the use of a student-friendly scale; (2) setting personal goals related to their own learning based on a proficiency scale; and (3) explaining how class activities and assignments relate to a proficiency scale.

Reflecting on Learning and Performance

The language of learning targets on proficiency scales is typically very appropriate for teachers, but may not have a lot of meaning to students. This is simply a function of the standards upon which scales are based. Standards are not developed for students themselves. Therefore, it is often beneficial to create student-friendly versions of proficiency scales. There are a few common practices when generating a student-friendly proficiency scale, including the following.

- Change the beginning words of each learning target on the scale from "The student will" to "I can." This makes the scale feel more personal to students.

- Remove any unnecessary explanatory language from the proficiency scale. This includes descriptors of performance often included on the teacher version, such as "There are no major errors or omissions regarding the simpler details and processes."

- Exercise formatting options that make the scale more user-friendly for the student, such as checklists. Other examples of this practice include highlighting the most important words on the scale, color coding levels on the scale, and including images that relate to specific learning targets.

The following vignette addresses asking students to reflect on their own learning through the use of a student-friendly scale.

Mr. Jameson teaches English 9 at Glendale High School. He and the other two English 9 teachers have scales that provide great clarity for them as teachers regarding what students need to know and be able to do, but the scales are not conducive for use with students. Therefore, Mr. Jameson and his colleagues create a student-friendly version of each scale. Figure 4.7 is an example of one of their student-friendly proficiency scales.

This ELA teacher team has chosen to structure their student-friendly scales as checklists. They believe that this will help clarify for students what they know and what they still need to learn. They have agreed to ask their students to reflect on their current level of performance on each scale no fewer than three times during the instructional unit so that students can observe their own growth over time.

Kolby is a student in Mr. Jameson's English 9 class. The class is just beginning the unit of instruction on analyzing ideas and themes, so Mr. Jameson asks students to reflect on each learning target on the proficiency scale

Content Area: English Language Arts **Grade Level:** 9–10 **Title of Scale:** Analyzing Ideas and Themes

Score 4.0: Complex Content

Demonstrations of learning that go above and beyond what was explicitly taught

For example, **I can:**

☐ Decide which of several possible themes in a text is the strongest

Score 3.0: Target Content

The expectations for all learners

I can:

☐ Determine the main ideas or themes in a text

☐ Describe the development of an idea or theme over the course of a text

Score 2.0: Simple Content

Foundational knowledge, simpler procedures, isolated details, vocabulary

I can recognize or recall specific vocabulary, such as:

☐ *detail*, *main idea*, *theme*, *topic*

I can perform basic processes, such as:

☐ Identify important details and claims in a text, including repeated details

☐ Describe how repeated details change over the course of a text

☐ List common themes found in literature

I can recognize or recall specific vocabulary, such as:

☐ *character*, *event*, *paragraph*, *section*

I can perform basic processes, such as:

☐ Explain how specific words strengthen a main idea or theme

☐ Explain how specific sections of a text strengthen a main idea or theme

☐ Identify the attitudes of particular characters toward a main idea or theme

Score 1.0

With help, **I can** perform score 2.0 and 3.0 expectations.

Source: Adapted from Simms, 2016.

Figure 4.7: A student-friendly scale for English, grade 9.

and check off learning targets they already know. Since the class has only just started learning about this topic, Kolby checks off a few of the score 2.0 learning targets that he recalls from previous classes.

Mr. Jameson asks students to perform this reflection again at a later point during the unit of instruction, and again at the end of the unit.

When asked about this practice, Kolby shares: "When I reflect on the learning targets on the scale, I gain clarity about what I already know and what I don't know yet. It helps me as a learner to focus on the stuff I still need to learn. It also motivates me to keep working hard when I see my knowledge grow related to something I really need to learn."

Setting Goals

Another student use of proficiency scales is personal goal setting. In *A Teacher's Guide to Standards-Based Learning,* Heflebower and her colleagues (2019) stated:

> Goal setting is an integral part of a standards-based learning environment because it helps focus students on individual needs related to specific learning targets, and because the most important and influential instructional decisions are often made by learners themselves (Stiggins, 2008). Goal setting and tracking progress go hand-in-hand. As students set goals, they track progress about those standards-based learning targets. In turn, tracking progress provides students with information regarding their initial goals, and often will assist them in modifying the goal or creating a new one. (p. 47)

Consider Kolby's initial reflection from the previous vignette. Since this took place at the beginning of the instructional unit for Analyzing Ideas and Themes, it is a perfect time for him and his classmates to set a personal goal related to this proficiency scale. Kolby's personal learning goal might be as follows:

> *Currently, I am performing at 1.5 on the proficiency scale for analyzing ideas and themes. My goal is to achieve score 3.0 on this scale. In order to achieve my goal, I will seek extra help on assignments when needed, pay close attention during class activities, turn all assignments in on time, and reread text for deep understanding.*

Numerous positive outcomes result when this type of student goal setting occurs. First of all, the student has personally identified the level of learning he or she wants to attain, which may lead the student to engaging more fully in the learning opportunities. Secondly, the student has identified actions he or she will take to meet the goal. The student's motivation to follow through on these tasks will likely be stronger because he or she

made those decisions independently. Finally, this goal-setting process positions the student to track his or her own progress, which Marzano (2017) considered "one of the most powerful uses of a proficiency scale because it allows students to see their growth along a continuum of knowledge" (p. 14). Figure 4.8 is an example of a goal setting and tracking progress form.

Explaining How Assignments Relate to Learning Goals

Finally, the use of proficiency scales in the classroom can help students see the connection between learning targets on the proficiency scale and the activities and assignments that are part of daily opportunities to learn. Many learners question why they have to complete a certain assignment at a given time. Absent this understanding, some learners believe that a teacher gives assignments to keep learners busy and quiet, or that assignments are given merely so that grades can be established for report card purposes.

In a classroom where scales are the basis of instruction and learning, the teacher strives to build students' understanding that activities and assignments are opportunities to increase knowledge related to a learning target on a scale. In order to form this understanding, learners need to see the relationship between each activity or assignment and specific language on a scale. Therefore, it is helpful for a teacher to explicate this connection for students initially. A teacher may say something like, "Today I am asking you to complete the matching activity for text features to ensure you are able to do the second learning target on our text features proficiency scale."

A second means of making this connection is to ask students why they are participating in a particular activity. If a student is able to respond, "This activity will help me master the second learning target on the proficiency scale," he or she has clearly made the connection between the scale and activities or assignments.

Name: _____

AP ENGLISH LITERATURE

Goal Setting and Tracking Progress

Essential Learning for 1.AP Literacy Analysis: The learner is able to analyze, interpret, and evaluate texts in a variety of genres and from a variety of literary periods from the 16th to the 21st century.

Current Score (out of 4) _____ Goal _____ by _____ (date)

In order to accomplish the above goal, I will do the following:

☐ Class discussion	☐ Extra help from teacher	☐ Complete homework
☐ Attend study group	☐ Study with a peer	☐ Other (approved by teacher)

Goal Tracking:

4								
3								
2								
1								
0								
	A	**B**	**C**	**D**	**E**	**F**	**G**	**H**

Assessments:

A. _____ B. _____ C. _____ D. _____

E. _____ F. _____ G. _____ H. _____

Source: © 2012 by Jeff Flygare. Used with permission.

Figure 4.8: Goal setting and tracking progress form.

The following vignette showcases a school where students learned about how scales benefit them as learners.

Carver Elementary began the work of proficiency scale development in 2015. Since then, teachers have worked diligently to use the scales consistently in their classrooms. While some teachers seem comfortable with using proficiency scales for various purposes, others are still struggling to understand what they should do or what they should ask their students to do in relation to the proficiency scales. So, Mr. Jackson, the building principal, facilitates a collaborative process at a Friday afternoon professional development session.

Mr. Jackson asks teachers to work as grade-level teams to identify teacher and student action statements that clarify what it looks like and sounds like when scales are the center of classroom interactions. When the teacher teams finish this identification process, he brings them together to compare lists and determine, as an entire staff, which statements they want everyone to use as guidance. The following is a checklist of teacher and student action steps generated by the collective group of teachers.

continued ⇨

Teacher Action Steps

❑ The teacher has a proficiency scale posted so that all students can see it.

❑ The teacher makes reference to the proficiency scale throughout the lesson.

❑ The teacher overviews the proficiency scale for students at the beginning of the instructional unit.

❑ The teacher asks students to reflect on the proficiency scale to determine their current level of performance.

❑ The teacher asks students to explain the meaning of the levels on the proficiency scale.

❑ The teacher helps students understand how the assignments and activities relate to the proficiency scale.

❑ The teacher assesses students on the learning targets within the levels on the scale.

Student Action Steps

❑ When asked, students can explain the learning target for the lesson.

❑ When asked, students can explain how their current activities and assignments relate to the learning target or targets on a proficiency scale.

❑ When asked, students can explain the meaning of the levels of performance on the proficiency scale.

❑ When asked, students can explain the purpose for reflecting on their current level of performance on the proficiency scale.

❑ When asked, students can determine a personal goal for learning related to a proficiency scale.

❑ When asked, students can track their progress to a personal goal.

These checklists help teachers understand how they should use proficiency scales in their classrooms, as well as what students should be able to do or explain. It also helps ensure consistency in the school with respect to how teachers build students' understanding of scales.

*Visit **MarzanoResources.com/reproducibles** to download a free reproducible version of the checklists from this vignette.*

Parent Use of Proficiency Scales

When a school begins using proficiency scales, it is imperative that educators—individually and as a group—work diligently to build parents' and other caregivers' understanding of scales. For many parents, the concept of a proficiency scale will be brand new; most have no personal experience with scales or their use. Scales communicate to everyone involved in the learning process what all students must know and be able to do. Because this information is so essential to understanding what students will experience in the classroom, educators should pay significant and consistent attention to ensuring that all stakeholders understand the key concepts.

Informing parents about proficiency scales can occur in a variety of ways. Some schools send a letter of explanation to each student's parents or guardians. This typically occurs very early in the school year so that when a student talks about or even brings home a proficiency scale, his or her parents will already have some knowledge about scales. Other schools create a brochure or other document to share information with parents. This communication tool would be distributed to parents at functions such as beginning-of-the-year open houses or parent-teacher conferences. Information about and even an example of a proficiency scale would appear in this publication. Figure 4.9 displays a scale that might appear in a brochure for parents describing the levels of the scale.

Another idea that some schools implement is to ask students to create their own proficiency scale and then to explain to their parents or guardians

The Levels of the Proficiency Scale		
Score 4.0	Advanced	A 4.0 indicates the student has advanced understanding and exceeds grade-level expectations. A student receiving a score of 4.0 demonstrates academically superior skills on that specific topic. This student shows initiative, challenges himself or herself, and provides evidence of advanced knowledge or skill. Not all students will attain this level on the scale.
Score 3.5	Progressing Toward Advanced	
Score 3.0	Proficient	A 3.0 indicates the student has proficient understanding and meets grade-level expectations. We want all of our students to reach this level on the scale. A student receiving a score of 3.0 is right on track with our academic expectations.
Score 2.5	Progressing Toward Proficient	
Score 2.0	Basic	A 2.0 indicates the student has basic understanding and is partially proficient at meeting grade-level expectations. A student receiving a 2.0 understands the basic concepts or skills, but has not yet reached the proficient level. A 2.0 should indicate that the student's performance varies in consistency with regard to accuracy, quality, and level of support needed.
Score 1.5	Progressing Toward Basic	
Score 1.0	Beginning	A 1.0 indicates the student has minimal understanding and needs significant guidance and support to show what he or she knows about the content on the scale.

Figure 4.9: Informing parents about proficiency scales.

what scales are and how they are used. Heflebower and her colleagues (2019) stated:

> Students who clearly understand proficiency scales and how they relate to grades can often help educate their parents. One strategy is to have students create their own proficiency scales that demonstrate the progressions of learning for a self-selected aspect of their life. This gives students a personal connection and understanding about what a proficiency scale is and how it relates to their own development of a process or skill. Students can use the scale they create to communicate the concept of proficiency scales to their parents without having academic content involved. (p. 124)

Figure 4.10 (page 56) is an example of such a scale.

While there is more than one right way to communicate with parents about proficiency scales, it is critical that information about these important tools is provided in an ongoing manner.

Once parents understand proficiency scales, they can use these tools in multiple ways. First, scales become a means for parents to know what their child must learn by the end of a school year or course. This means that parents should have access to proficiency scales, either hard copies or online. In the case of the grade 2 example, parents would know that using text features is a nonnegotiable skill for their child, along with the other content showcased in various grade 2 English language arts proficiency scales. When parents have this information, they can support learning in a variety of ways at home, which enhances the partnership between home and school.

4.0 Advanced	I can dribble a basketball between my legs and behind my back while running up the court.
3.0 Proficient	I can dribble a basketball with either hand while running up the court. I can dribble a basketball back and forth between hands while running up the court.
2.0 Progressing	I can dribble a basketball with my right hand while walking. I can dribble a basketball with my left hand while walking. I can dribble back and forth between my right and left hands while walking.

Source: Heflebower et al., 2019, p. 125.

Figure 4.10: A student-created proficiency scale.

Knowledge of and access to proficiency scales also enable parents to initiate communication with teachers about their children's current levels of performance and request ideas for how they can provide additional support at home. They also ensure that ongoing, meaningful conversations can occur between parents and students regarding the current instructional focus. Parents can regularly check in with students about how they are doing with the content. They can also remind their children about the importance of nonacademic behaviors that are the subject of scales (see chapter 7, page 89). Perhaps most importantly, knowledge and use of proficiency scales provide parents a means for giving meaningful feedback and celebrating learning. When support for learning content occurs both at school and home, it seems logical that everyone involved reaps the benefits.

We have discussed uses of proficiency scales by teachers, students, and parents. When these tools are implemented in a school or classroom, it makes sense to use scales to enhance grading practices as well. Some teachers, teams of teachers, schools, and even districts provide information about learning to students and their parents through a process called *standards-based grading*. In this system, current performance relative to proficiency scales is recorded on the formal report card. For more information about this practice, consult *A School Leader's Guide to Standards-Based Grading* (Heflebower et al., 2014) or *A Teacher's Guide to Standards-Based Learning* (Heflebower et al., 2019).

Summary

This chapter presents information about proficiency scale use by teachers, students, and parents. For teachers, proficiency scales are the foundation of curriculum, instruction, assessment, and feedback—perhaps the majority of what takes place in the classroom. For students, proficiency scales enable increased ownership of learning through reflection, goal setting, and understanding the purpose of various assignments. Parents also use scales to stay informed about what their children need to learn during any academic year or course. This knowledge helps them support learners outside of the school environment. While there are different uses of proficiency scales depending on who the user is, all stakeholders benefit from their use and the resulting clarity about what students must know and be able to do by the end of a grade level or course. The next chapter will provide information about useful classroom tools related to proficiency scales—rubrics, criteria checklists, and pacing guides.

Chapter 4 Comprehension Questions

1. How might a teacher use a proficiency scale?

2. What are some ways students can use a proficiency scale?

3. How are proficiency scales important to parents of learners?

CHAPTER 5
Scales and Related Tools

While this book clearly focuses on proficiency scales, it is important for educators to understand the relationship between proficiency scales and other classroom tools. Specifically, we will discuss rubrics, criteria checklists, and pacing guides. All are valuable tools—proficiency scales will enhance their use rather than eliminate them. A scale and a rubric, for example, can work interdependently to offer comprehensive and accurate feedback to a learner on priority content. This chapter will provide information and examples of how proficiency scales combine with other tools to improve curriculum, instruction, assessment, and feedback.

Rubrics

A rubric is a criterion-based evaluation tool that teachers use to give students feedback on a performance task or project (McTighe, 2017). While proficiency scales define a progression of knowledge or skill, rubrics describe levels of performance on a specific assignment. As such, proficiency scales and rubrics work well together, with scales providing a broader perspective on learning and rubrics taking a closer look at one piece of evidence. In this section, we will discuss two types of rubrics and explore how teachers can utilize scales and rubrics in combination.

Two Types of Rubrics

Rubrics are suited well for open-ended learning opportunities, because these tasks do not have a single correct answer or solution the way a multiple-choice question or a math problem does. Jay McTighe (2013), author and expert on rubrics, described two types of rubrics:

> Two general types of rubrics—holistic and analytic—are widely used to judge student products and performances. A holistic rubric provides an overall impression of a student's work. Holistic rubrics yield a single score or rating for a product or performance. An analytic rubric divides a product or performance into distinct traits or dimensions and judges each separately. Since an analytic rubric rates each of the identified traits independently, a separate score is provided for each. (p. 91)

First, we will discuss holistic rubrics. Suppose that a fourth-grade classroom includes the following priority science standard: "The student will use the scientific method to conduct an experiment." Part of the scientific method includes data collection, display, and analysis, so after students design and conduct their experiment and collect data, their teacher asks them to represent their findings on graphs of their choosing. The teacher has designed a holistic rubric, shown in figure 5.1 (page 60), and presents the rubric to students so that they will

59

understand the success criteria for their data displays. The criteria in the rubric not only provide the basis for evaluation of the students' products, they serve as teaching and learning targets as well.

Data Display	
3	• Data are represented accurately on the graph. • All elements of the graph are correctly labelled. • The graph has an appropriate title.
2	• Data are represented on the graph, but minor errors exist. • Some elements of the graph are labelled correctly, but errors exist or labels are missing. • The graph has a title, but it lacks clear alignment to the information displayed.
1	• Data are represented incorrectly, contain errors, or are missing. • Few elements of the graph are labelled correctly, or labels are missing. • The graph title is not related to the data displayed, or a title is missing.

Source: Adapted from McTighe, 2017, p. 7. Used with permission.

Figure 5.1: Holistic rubric for data display assignments.

Most teachers like holistic rubrics because they are relatively easy to use and result in a single score for the task. This type of rubric is also useful when helping a student understand how to improve his or her work product. For example, suppose that one learner submits a data display that meets two of the three criteria at level 3. A teacher can easily inform the student about how to improve his or her work by identifying the criteria that are lacking. The teacher might say to the student:

Your graph has an appropriate title, and all of the elements are correctly labelled, but if you look carefully, you will see that you have a couple of minor errors in the data represented on your graph. If you can find and fix these errors, your data display will be better.

One challenge with holistic rubrics is that they tend to include subjective descriptors (for example, *some*, *appropriate*), which can make it difficult for teachers to assign scores consistently and fairly. It is also important to note again that educators would not use this rubric to score student proficiency on the entire priority standard. Instead, this holistic rubric provides information to the teacher about student performance on the specific task for which it was designed.

The second type of rubric—the analytic rubric—provides more detailed information than a holistic rubric because it describes specific components of the performance or task independently of one another. While all content areas can utilize analytic rubrics, they are very common in English language arts and world languages when students are asked to write, speak, and listen. Additionally, content areas such as art, music, and physical education include prominent use of analytic rubrics.

When developing or selecting a rubric for a specific performance or task, it is important that teachers spend adequate time identifying the specific feedback components. It is very common for a rubric to include three to five components. For example, consider a high school world language classroom where teachers have identified the following priority standard: "The student will communicate information about multiple topics using phrases, simple sentences, and memorized questions." The world language teachers have worked collaboratively to develop an analytic rubric (see figure 5.2) for offering students feedback when they use the language to communicate in the classroom. The rubric describes four levels of performance for various components of interpersonal speaking, including speaking comprehensibly, understanding what others say, and using accurate grammar and vocabulary. Teachers will use this rubric to rate specific instances of communication, and they will consider performance on this rubric as one piece of evidence when making decisions regarding student performance on the priority standard as a whole.

INTERPERSONAL SPEAKING

	4 Exceeds Expectations	3 Meets Expectations	2 Approaches Expectations	1 Below Expectations
Task How well do I complete the task?	• I complete the task by creating a variety of statements and questions. • I respond fully and appropriately to all or almost all parts of the prompt. • My ideas are supported with examples and elaboration.	• I complete the task by using learned statements and questions. • I respond adequately to most parts of the prompt. • My ideas are supported with some examples.	• I complete the task by using some simple learned statements and questions. • I respond inadequately to some parts of the prompt. • My ideas are supported with few examples.	• I complete the task by using memorized words and high-frequency phrases. • I respond inadequately to most parts of the prompt. • My ideas are not supported with examples.
Comprehensibility How well do others understand me?	• I can be easily understood. • The message is clear (pronunciation and volume).	• I can be understood. • The message is mostly clear (pronunciation and volume).	• I can be somewhat understood. • The message is partially clear (volume and pronunciation).	• I can be understood only with great effort. • The message is not clear (volume and pronunciation).
Comprehension How well do I understand others?	• I can easily understand a variety of sentences and questions. • I rarely need repetition.	• I can understand a variety of simple questions and answers. • I sometimes need repetition.	• I can understand some simple questions and answers. • I often need repetition.	• I can understand memorized words and some high-frequency phrases. • I often need repetition.
Vocabulary Use How extensive and applicable is my vocabulary?	• I consistently use extensive vocabulary to complete the task.	• I use adequate vocabulary to complete the task.	• I use limited or repetitive vocabulary.	• I use extremely limited or repetitive vocabulary. • My native language interferes.
Language Control How accurate is my language?	• I correctly use grammatical structures appropriate to the task most of the time. • I demonstrate emerging use of verb tenses and some advanced grammatical structures. • Errors do not interfere.	• I use grammatical structures appropriate to the task most of the time. • Errors rarely interfere.	• I use grammatical structures appropriate to the task some of the time. • Errors occasionally interfere.	• I rarely use grammatical structures appropriate to the task. • Errors frequently interfere.
Fluency and Communication Strategies How well do I keep the conversation going?	• I keep the conversation going with very few pauses. • I ask for clarification in a variety of ways.	• I keep the conversation going with a few pauses. • I sometimes ask for clarification.	• I keep the conversation going with some pauses. • I often ask for clarification.	• I have some difficulty keeping the conversation going. • I have frequent pauses.

Source: © 2016 by Laramie County School District 1. Used with permission.

Figure 5.2: Analytic rubric for interpersonal speaking.

Joint Use of Scales and Rubrics

Now that we understand holistic and analytic rubrics, let's examine the similarities, differences, and interactions between a rubric and a proficiency scale. Table 5.1 presents key points of comparison.

Table 5.1: Comparison of Rubrics and Proficiency Scales

Similarities Between a Rubric and a Proficiency Scale	
• Both are tools that are used for offering feedback to learners. • Both have scores associated with multiple levels of performance. • Both provide clear understanding of expectations for performance. • Both may be provided to learners at the beginning of a learning opportunity.	

Differences Between a Rubric and a Proficiency Scale	
Rubric	**Proficiency Scale**
Developed for a specific product, project, or task	Developed for a broader conceptual understanding of a priority standard or topic
Used for evaluating performance on a specific product, project, or task	Used for evaluating progress on a priority standard or topic
Used to communicate critical components of a specific product, project, or task	Used as a framework for instruction related to a priority standard or topic
Often includes qualitative or quantitative language (*sometimes, always, frequent, consistent*)	Includes language that articulates what a student must know and be able to do
May be used as an assessment tool	Used as a framework for classroom assessment practices

In addition to understanding how rubrics and proficiency scales are alike and different, it is important to understand how teachers might use both tools together to determine student performance on a priority standard. Consider a seventh-grade team where three teachers have developed proficiency scales for all priority standards. One of the seventh-grade priority standards is "The student will write grade-appropriate arguments to support claims with clear reasons and relevant evidence" (NGA & CCSSO, 2010a; W.7.1). The corresponding proficiency scale appears in figure 5.3.

As is typical, classroom instruction related to this priority standard begins at score 2.0. In the case of the argumentative writing scale, there is some academic vocabulary that students need to know. Additionally, students must learn about what constitutes effective argumentative writing before being asked to write an argumentative essay. In order for this to happen, the teacher might provide a list of attributes of effective argumentative writing. He or she may provide numerous examples of argumentative writing to students and establish a protocol for identifying this type of writing. Once the teacher has adequate evidence that students have grasped the score 2.0 content, the class can move to the score 3.0 learning target. Here, the teacher introduces a rubric for argumentative writing tasks, as shown in figure 5.4 (page 64). The seventh-grade teacher team also developed this analytic rubric together, and they will use it in their classrooms to assess students' individual argumentative writing assignments.

The seventh-grade team has chosen to develop an analytic rubric. In their professional judgment, effective argumentative writing includes three critical components: (1) statement of purpose and focus, (2) organization, and (3) elaboration of evidence. This team of teachers has included two additional components of writing on their rubric: (1) language and vocabulary and (2) conventions. While these two components are very important, they are not

ARGUMENTATIVE WRITING		
Grade 7		
Score 4.0	In addition to score 3.0 performance, the student demonstrates in-depth inferences and applications that go beyond what was taught. For example, the student will: • Acknowledge and counter opposing claims, as appropriate	
	Score 3.5	**In addition to score 3.0 performance, partial success at score 4.0 content**
Score 3.0	The student will: • Write grade-appropriate arguments to support claims with clear reasons and relevant evidence (W.7.1)	
	Score 2.5	No major errors or omissions regarding score 2.0 content, and partial success at score 3.0 content
Score 2.0	The student will recognize or recall specific vocabulary, such as: • *argument, claim, concluding statement, credible, evidence, reasoning, source, support* The student will perform basic processes, such as: • Identify the characteristics of a well-written argument • Write arguments using a teacher-provided template	
	Score 1.5	Partial success at score 2.0 content, and major errors or omissions regarding score 3.0 content
Score 1.0	With help, partial success at score 2.0 content and score 3.0 content	
	Score 0.5	With help, partial success at score 2.0 content but not at score 3.0 content
Score 0.0	Even with help, no success	

Source: Adapted from Marzano et al., 2013, p. 131.

Figure 5.3: Proficiency scale for argumentative writing, grade 7.

specific to argumentative writing. For this reason, they will be used to give students feedback on their written products but will not be included in the feedback on or assessment of their proficiency with argumentation. Each of the five components has been described in four levels on the analytic rubric.

Prior to giving students the task of writing an argumentative essay, each teacher reviews the scoring rubric with his or her entire class. The teachers also provide paper copies of the rubric to students, as the information presented on the rubric will be helpful to them as they write their essays. Once students write and turn in their essays, the teachers will use the rubric to determine the quality of each student's work. Ultimately, they will use each student's

performance on this assignment, as described by the rubric, as one piece of evidence in the decision about current levels of performance on the proficiency scale for argumentative writing. Table 5.2 (page 66) shows one class of seventh-grade students and their performance on the argumentative writing scoring rubric. In making a decision about each student's overall score, the teacher considers each rubric component and makes a judgment about the most appropriate overall score.

While a single performance does not dictate a student's score level on the proficiency scale, scores on a rubric help the teacher consider whether or not a student has mastered the learning target at score 3.0. In essence, the rubric is a tool that offers

Argumentative Writing Scoring Rubric

Score	Statement of Purpose and Focus	Organization	Elaboration of Evidence	Language and Vocabulary	Conventions
4.0	The response is fully sustained and consistently and purposefully focused: • Claim is clearly stated, focused, and strongly maintained • Claim is introduced and communicated clearly within the context	The response has a clear and effective organizational structure creating unity and completeness: • Effective, consistent use of a variety of transitional strategies • Logical progression of ideas from beginning to end • Effective introduction and conclusion for audience and purpose • Strong connections among ideas, with some syntactic variety	The response provides thorough and convincing support and evidence for the writer's claim that includes the effective use of sources, facts, and details. The response achieves substantial depth that is specific and relevant: • Use of evidence from sources is smoothly integrated, comprehensive, relevant, and concrete • Effective use of a variety of elaborative techniques	The response clearly and effectively expresses ideas, using precise language: • Use of academic and domain-specific vocabulary is clearly appropriate for the audience and purpose	The response demonstrates a strong command of conventions: • Few, if any, errors are present in usage and sentence formation • Effective and consistent use of punctuation, capitalization, and spelling
3.0	The response is adequately sustained and generally focused: • Claim is clear and for the most part maintained, though some loosely related material may be present • Context provided for the claim is adequate	The response has an evident organizational structure and a sense of completeness, though there may be minor flaws and some ideas may be loosely connected: • Adequate use of transitional strategies with some variety • Adequate progression of ideas from beginning to end • Adequate introduction and conclusion • Adequate, if slightly inconsistent, connection among ideas	The response provides adequate support and evidence for writer's claim that includes the use of sources, facts, and details. The response achieves some depth and specificity but is predominantly general: • Some evidence from sources is integrated, though citations may be general or imprecise • Adequate use of some elaborative techniques	The response adequately expresses ideas, employing a mix of precise with more general language: • Use of domain-specific vocabulary is generally appropriate for the audience and purpose	The response demonstrates an adequate command of conventions: • Some errors in usage and sentence formation may be present, but no systematic pattern of errors is displayed • Adequate use of punctuation, capitalization, and spelling

2.0	The response is somewhat sustained and may have a minor drift in focus: • May be clearly focused on the claim, but is insufficiently sustained • Claim on the issue may be somewhat unclear and unfocused	The response has an inconsistent organizational structure, and flaws are evident: • Inconsistent use of basic transitional strategies with little variety • Uneven progression of ideas from beginning to end • Conclusion and introduction, if present, are weak • Weak connection among ideas	The response provides uneven, cursory support and evidence for the writer's claim that includes partial or uneven use of sources, facts, and details, and achieves little depth: • Evidence from sources is weakly integrated, and citations, if present, are uneven • Weak or uneven use of elaborative techniques	The response expresses ideas unevenly, using simplistic language: • Use of domain-specific vocabulary may at times be inappropriate for the audience and purpose	
1.0	The response may be related to the purpose but may offer little relevant detail: • May be very brief • May have a major drift • Claim may be confusing or ambiguous	The response has little or no discernible organizational structure: • Few or no transitional strategies are evident • Frequent extraneous ideas may intrude	The response provides minimal support and evidence for the writer's claim that includes little or no use of sources, facts, and details: • Use of evidence from sources is minimal, absent, in error, or irrelevant	The response expression of ideas is vague, lacks clarity, or is confusing: • Uses little language or domain-specific vocabulary • May have little sense of audience and purpose	

Source: Smarter Balanced Assessment Consortium, 2012.

Figure 5.4: Analytic rubric for argumentative writing tasks.

students feedback on a specific task encompassed within a score level on a proficiency scale.

This process is applicable in any classroom where performance tasks are the best means for a teacher to learn about what a student knows and is able to do. As another example, consider the very generic art proficiency scale in figure 5.5 (page 66). With this generic scale, a rubric offers the necessary details related to any specific task the student is asked to complete. Suppose a high school art class is working on drawing for a portion of a nine-week period. After providing the appropriate instruction, the teacher assigns a drawing task. Before asking

students to complete the task, he or she presents the scoring rubric that will be used to determine the quality of the drawing project. Figure 5.6 (page 67) shows a rubric specific to the drawing task.

Just as in the previous writing example, performance on this particular assignment will not necessarily be the same score that the teacher assigns at the end of the grading period. However, the student's performance on this rubric will be an indicator as to how the student is performing on the proficiency scale. The performance on the rubric informs the performance on the proficiency scale.

Table 5.2: Class Scores on a Rubric

Student	Statement of Purpose and Focus	Organization	Elaboration of Evidence	Overall Score
A	2	2	2	2
B	3	2	2	2.5
C	3	3	3	3
D	3	4	3	3
E	4	4	4	4
F	2	2	2	2
G	2	3	3	2.5
H	3	3	3	3
I	3	4	3	3
J	4	3	4	3.5
K	2	2	1	2
L	3	3	3	3
M	4	3	3	3
N	4	3	4	3.5
O	3	3	3	3
P	2	3	3	2.5
Q	3	3	3	3
R	4	4	4	4

Criteria Checklists

A checklist is another tool that is often useful for offering students meaningful feedback. Like a rubric, a checklist provides specific criteria for success on a task or a performance. Different from a rubric, a checklist doesn't present various levels of performance. Instead, it provides a list of desired behaviors or elements of performance.

As previously stated, one of the primary purposes for engaging in proficiency scale development is to ensure clear understanding of what all students need to know and be able to do. Interestingly, criteria checklists can aid in this process in two ways—either based on or as the basis of a scale. Some schools choose to begin their scale development process by identifying success criteria related to priority standards. While success criteria and proficiency scales are not the same thing,

FUNDAMENTALS OF ART	
ADVANCED Score 4.0	In addition to score 3.0, the student demonstrates in-depth inferences and applications that go beyond what was taught.
PROFICIENT Score 3.0	The student demonstrates mastery of class-level skills and processes with no major errors or omissions.
BASIC Score 2.0	The student demonstrates mastery of all basic skills and processes and partial mastery of the higher-level skills and processes with no major errors or omissions.
BEGINNING Score 1.0	The student requires help to partially complete class-level skills and processes and some of the more complex ideas and processes.
NYA Not yet assessed	There is not sufficient evidence to assess student progress at this time.

Figure 5.5: Fundamentals of art proficiency scale.

	Advanced	Proficient	Basic	Beginning
Craftsmanship	Artwork is impeccable and shows no evidence of smudge marks, rips, tears, or folds. No erasure lines showing	Artwork is neat and shows very little evidence of smudge marks, rips, tears, or folds. A few erasure lines showing	Artwork is somewhat messy and shows either smudge marks or rips, tears, or folds. Some erasure lines showing	Artwork is messy and shows smudge marks and rips, tears, or folds. Erasure lines showing
Techniques and Art Concepts	Artwork shows a mastery of advanced techniques in composition. All objects are placed in correct space. Negative and positive space is balanced. Paper is completely drawn on and shows a background, mid-ground, and foreground.	Artwork shows good technique. All objects are placed in correct space. Negative and positive space is almost balanced. Paper is drawn on leaving some area undone and shows a background, mid-ground, and foreground.	Artwork shows some technique and understanding of art concepts. Average use of negative and positive space Paper is half filled, and foreground and background are clearly shown.	Artwork lacks technique and understanding of art concepts. Paper is left mainly blank; little area drawn on and does not show a background, mid-ground, or foreground.
Creativity	Artwork reflects a high level of originality. Student uses line, shading, or form in a highly original manner.	Artwork reflects originality. Student uses line, shading, or form in an original manner.	Artwork shows some evidence of originality. Student uses line, shading, or form in a slightly original manner.	Artwork shows little or no evidence of original thought. Student does not use line, shading, or form in a creative manner.
Shading and Proportion	Completed artwork is fully shaded showing excellent placement of light and darks using excellent drawing technique. Still-life objects are in excellent proportion with real-life objects.	Completed artwork is almost fully shaded showing good placement of light and darks using good drawing technique. Still-life objects are mostly in good proportion with real-life objects.	Completed artwork is half shaded showing average placement of light and darks using average drawing technique. Some still-life objects are in proportion with real-life objects.	Completed artwork is not shaded or incorrectly shaded. Still-life objects are incorrect in proportion with real-life objects.

Figure 5.6: Rubric for drawing.

identification of success criteria can be an effective first step of scale development. Table 5.3 (page 68) displays similarities and differences between a proficiency scale and success criteria.

As an example, in order to provide clarity to students about what they need to know and be able to do, Hampton Public School in Hampton, Nebraska chose to have teachers identify success criteria. Superintendent Holly Herzberg reflected on this process:

> Our district knew we needed to get clarity in place about what all kids need to know and be able to do. However, we just didn't feel the timing was right to tackle proficiency scales. So, we decided to start with success criteria. We feel very positively about

Table 5.3: Comparison of Proficiency Scales and Success Criteria

Similarities Between a Proficiency Scale and Success Criteria
• Both relate to a priority standard or a learning target that must be mastered by all students. • Both provide clarity for teachers and students. • Both are intended to be used during instruction and for assessment development.

Differences Between a Proficiency Scale and Success Criteria	
Proficiency Scale	**Success Criteria**
Articulates a progression of knowledge related to a priority standard or topic	Articulates statements of clarity related only to the level of the standard (no simple or complex content)

The student will tell and write time from analog and digital clocks to the nearest five minutes.

Proficiency Scale		Success Criteria
Score 4.0	The student will solve real-world problems involving elapsed time.	**The student will:** • Describe an analog and digital clock • Write time using the correct format • Tell time from digital clocks to the nearest five minutes • Tell time from analog clocks to the nearest five minutes
Score 3.0	The student will tell time on analog and digital clocks to the nearest five minutes.	
Score 2.0	The student will count by fives to sixty. The student will tell time to the nearest hour, half-hour, and quarter-hour. The student will identify the minute hand and the hour hand.	

Source: © 2016 by South Sioux City Community Schools. Used with permission.

this first step. When I walk into a classroom and see the success criteria for a priority standard displayed and hear them being referenced by teachers and students, I know they are making an impact on students having clear understanding of what is important in second-grade math, sixth-grade social studies, or English 11. (personal communication, December 7, 2018)

Desiree Christenson is a sixth-grade teacher at Hampton Public School. She has worked diligently to identify success criteria for each of the prioritized standards for ELA and mathematics in order to provide clarity for herself and her students. Desiree shared how this has impacted her classroom:

Implementing learning targets and success criteria has completely streamlined and focused my instruction. My instructional planning has an increased sense of purpose and clarity. I am more intentional as I sift through the curriculum, making sure that what I use clearly aligns with the learning targets that make up the success criteria. Identifying success criteria has also helped me assess learning. Since I now have what needs to be learned clearly articulated, it is easier for me to see where students are in the learning process. Using the criteria, I can think about how to best help each student learn the content.

I've always wanted my students to go home and talk about what they learned in school that day. Because the identified success criteria are used daily, I am confident that they are able to do this more easily and with a higher degree of accuracy than ever before. (personal communication, February 3, 2019)

While the process of identifying success criteria is certainly helpful to teachers and beneficial to learners, a proficiency scale is a more comprehensive document. Because a scale communicates a progression of knowledge, it provides stronger support for teachers as they strive to meet the instructional needs of all levels of learners. In this way, success criteria can serve as an interim or first step toward scales.

Alternatively, teachers or teams can develop checklists of success criteria to help operationalize an existing scale in their classrooms. The following vignette presents an example of how a checklist and a proficiency scale can help determine students' current level of performance.

Mr. Jacobsen, an elementary physical education teacher, is about to begin a soccer unit with his fifth-grade students. He typically begins each unit by sharing the proficiency scales that he will be addressing during the instructional unit. Almost all of his units include the scale in figure 5.7 for movement skills and patterns, a priority in fifth-grade physical education.

In addition to using this general scale, Mr. Jacobsen has developed a checklist of required skills for each of his units. He has completed this action step to attain clarity related to the phrase "grade-appropriate movement skills and patterns," which is within the score 3.0 learning target. He understands that movement skills and patterns is a very comprehensive category of skills, and that the skills required for a unit on soccer are not the same skills needed when basketball or badminton are the focus of the unit. So, he has spent significant time determining the three to five grade-appropriate skills that he will be watching for as students engage in the class activities for each unit. For example, the checklist of skills for his soccer unit includes the following.

❑ Dribbling—keeps the ball moving between feet

❑ Passing—stops, plants one foot on the ground, and kicks the ball using the inside of the free foot to target

❑ Receiving—plants one foot on the ground, and stops the ball with the inside of the other foot

❑ Throwing—places both hands on the outside of the ball, and overhand throws to the target

This checklist actually becomes a part of the proficiency scale at score 3.0 (see figure 5.8, page 70). This practice ensures that he can talk with students about the required soccer skills very easily. It also serves as a reminder to Mr. Jacobsen of the required skills he is watching for as he observes students participate in classroom activities.

Mr. Jacobsen states, "The use of a checklist as part of my proficiency scale for movement skills and patterns has worked really well. It helps me be clear in my mind about what skills I need to teach the students during any of my instructional units. It also ensures that the students know what skills they need to practice and learn during classroom activities. In a performance-based classroom environment, the use of a checklist along with a proficiency scale is sometimes really helpful. I like how the language on this scale in particular gains another level of clarity with the integration of the checklist."

GRADE 5 MOVEMENT SKILLS AND PATTERNS	
SCORE 4.0	In addition to score 3.0, the student demonstrates a higher level of performance or additional movement skills and patterns.
SCORE 3.0	The student demonstrates grade-appropriate movement skills and patterns in a variety of activities.
SCORE 2.0	The student demonstrates partial mastery of the score 3.0 required skills.
SCORE 1.0	The student requires help to partially master the score 3.0 required skills.

Figure 5.7: Proficiency scale for movement skills and patterns, grade 5.

GRADE 5 MOVEMENT SKILLS AND PATTERNS—SOCCER	
Score 4.0	• In addition to score 3.0, the student demonstrates a higher level of performance or additional movement skills and patterns.

Score 3.0	The student:
	• Demonstrates grade-appropriate movement skills and patterns in a variety of activities
	   ❑ Dribbling—keeps the ball moving between feet
	   ❑ Passing—stops, plants one foot on the ground, and kicks the ball using the inside of the free foot to target
	   ❑ Receiving—plants one foot on the ground, and stops the ball with the inside of the other foot
	   ❑ Throwing—places both hands on the outside of the ball, and overhand throws to the target

Score 2.0	The student: • Demonstrates partial mastery of the score 3.0 required skills
Score 1.0	The student: • Requires help to partially master the score 3.0 required skills

Figure 5.8: Proficiency scale for movement skills and patterns in soccer, grade 5.

Pacing Guides

Another tool that can be useful in combination with proficiency scales is a pacing guide, which is a document that displays the order for teaching the content and the approximate amount of instructional time to spend on each scale.

The pacing guide in figure 5.9 was developed by a team of high school mathematics teachers. They identified ten priority topics and developed a scale for each. This information appears in the left column, along with the approximate number of class periods that will be allocated to teaching the content on the scale. The standards encompassed within each priority topic are shown next, and then the unit in the primary resource (the textbook). Finally, the last columns specify in which quarter or quarters each topic will be taught and reinforced. Whether there is one teacher or multiple teaching this course, this document is extremely informational. It serves as guidance to ensure consistency across classrooms regarding what is taught and how much instructional time is spent on each

topic. It is important to note that total time allotted to the various topics does not account for the entire academic year. This allows for flexibility when necessary in individual classrooms, and for addressing content outside of the priority topics, as teachers deem appropriate.

The next example (figure 5.10, page 72) is a partial kindergarten pacing guide for English language arts. This example presents less information than the previous example, and in a different format. However, it makes clear to all classroom teachers during which quarter of the academic year each ELA priority standard will receive instructional focus.

Summary

This chapter described several tools that can enhance educators' use of proficiency scales. Rubrics, checklists, and pacing guides are all useful tools for instruction and providing meaningful feedback to learners. Rubrics—either holistic or analytic—typically describe levels of performance on a specific project, product, or demonstration.

Topics	Priority Standards or Indicators	Unit	Quarter Taught	Quarter Reinforced
Equations and Inequalities Fifteen to eighteen days	MA 11.22.g Solve linear and absolute value equations and inequalities.	1	First	Second, third, fourth
Functions Nine to eleven days	MA 11.2.1.b Analyze a relation to determine if it is a function given graphs, tables, or algebraic notation. MA 11.2.1.e Analyze and graph linear functions and inequalities (point-slope form, slope-intercept form, standard form, intercepts, rate of change, parallel and perpendicular lines, vertical and horizontal lines, and inequalities).	2	First, second	Second, third, fourth
Graphing Twelve to fifteen days	MA 11.2.1.e Analyze and graph linear functions and inequalities (point-slope form, slope-intercept form, standard form, intercepts, rate of change, parallel and perpendicular lines, vertical and horizontal lines, and inequalities).	3	Second	Second, third, fourth
Systems of Equations Nine to eleven days	MA 11.2.1.h Analyze and solve systems of two linear equations and inequalities in two variables algebraically and graphically.	4	Second	Second, third, fourth
Writing Equations Five to seven days	MA 11.4.2.e Develop linear equations for linear models to predict unobserved outcomes using the regression line and correlations coefficient with technology.	5	Third	Third, fourth
Exponents Fourteen to sixteen days	11.2.2.c Simplify algebraic expressions involving integer and fractional exponents.	6	Third	Third, fourth
Polynomials Six to eight days	MA 11.2.2.i Perform operations (addition, subtraction, multiplication, division) on polynomials.	7	Third	Fourth
Factoring Ten to twelve days	MA 11.2.2.i Perform operations (addition, subtraction, multiplication, division) on polynomials.	8	Fourth	Fourth
Radicals Twelve to fourteen days	Simplify radical expressions rationalizing the denominator. Add, subtract, and multiply radical expressions and solve with radical equations.	9	Fourth	Fourth
Data Analysis and Probability Three to five days	MA 11.4.3.c Determine if events are mutually exclusive and calculate their probabilities in either case. MA 11.2.3.f Describe the shape, identify any outliers, and determine the spread of a data set.	10	Fourth	Fourth

Source: © 2019 by Columbus Public Schools. Used with permission.

Figure 5.9: Pacing guide for a high school mathematics course.

Vocabulary

Pacing	Standard Number	Standard Description
Q3	LA 0.1.5.a	Examine word structure elements and word patterns to determine meaning (plural forms).
Q1-Q4	LA 0.1.5.c	Acquire new academic and content-specific grade-level vocabulary, relate to prior knowledge, and apply in new situations.
Q2	LA 0.1.5.d	Identify semantic relationships (for example, conceptual categories) to determine word relationships.

Comprehension

Pacing	Standard Number	Standard Description
Q3	LA 0.1.6.b	Identify elements of literary text (for example, characters, setting, events).
Q1	LA 0.1.6.f	Identify text features in print and digital informational text (bold).
Q1-Q2	LA 0.1.6.g	Identify the basic characteristics of literary and informational text.
Q2	LA 0.1.6.h	Make connections between own life and other cultures in literary and informational text (text-to-self).
Q2	LA 0.1.6.k	Identify different purposes for reading (for example, inform, enjoy).
Q2	LA 0.1.6.l	Build background knowledge and activate prior knowledge to identify text-to-self connections.
Q2	LA 0.1.6.n	Make predictions about a text using prior knowledge, pictures, illustrations, and titles.
Q2	LA 0.1.6.o	Respond to text (for example, verbally, in writing, or artistically).

Writing Process

Pacing	Standard Number	Standard Description
Q3	LA 0.2.1.b	Generate representations of ideas (for example, pictures, labels, letter strings, words, simple sentences) and organize ideas relevant to a topic.
Q4	LA 0.2.1.d	Compose simple, grammatically correct sentences.
Q3	LA 0.2.1.i	Use own words to relate information.

Source: © 2016 by South Sioux City Community Schools. Used with permission.

Figure 5.10: Pacing guide for kindergarten ELA priority standards.

There are also times when a checklist, rather than a rubric, may be useful for providing clarity to learners about what they need to know and be able to do, or for providing feedback. It is through the use of these important tools that students gain understanding of how to improve. Finally, we discussed pacing guides, which outline the order and timing of instruction throughout the school year. The next chapter will address using proficiency scales with exceptional learners.

Chapter 5 Comprehension Questions

1. What is the difference between a holistic and analytic rubric?

2. What is similar between a rubric and a proficiency scale? What is the difference between the two?

3. What are the similarities and differences between proficiency scales and success criteria checklists?

4. How might a checklist be used in tandem with a proficiency scale?

5. How would a teacher use proficiency scales and pacing guides interdependently?

CHAPTER 6

The Use of Scales With Exceptional Learners

The academic proficiency scales described in previous chapters will be appropriate for the majority of students in a classroom. However, there are some important considerations related to using proficiency scales with exceptional learners, which include three categories of students. Heflebower and her colleagues (2014) stated that there are "several distinct groups [defined] as exceptional for the purposes of schooling and education. These include students with disabilities, English learners, and gifted and talented students" (p. 71). This chapter provides suggestions for ensuring appropriate and successful use of proficiency scales for and with students in these groups.

A Common Misunderstanding

Before providing suggestions for using scales with exceptional learners, it is important to discuss score 1.0 on the proficiency scale. To review, a student who earns a score 1.0 needs help to demonstrate partial success with the score 2.0 or score 3.0 content. Examples of help include rephrasing questions, asking probing questions, and providing prompts or sentence starters. Score 1.0 can apply to *any* student in the classroom, including an exceptional learner. Because of the word *help* within this level on the proficiency scale, some people wrongly believe that

an exceptional learner can only attain a maximum score of 1.0. To ensure that exceptional learners work toward learning targets in ways that are appropriate for them, teachers provide accommodations or modifications.

The primary difference between a general education student receiving help and an exceptional learner's accommodations or modifications is the formal identification of the student into one of the three exceptional learner categories. For example, a student with a disability would have an individualized education plan (IEP). This plan denotes accommodations or modifications that, by law, teachers must provide in order for the learner to access the content being taught. It is important to note that the accommodations or modifications encompassed within an individual learner plan, such as an IEP, should always be the primary guidelines for supporting any individual exceptional learner. English learners and gifted and talented students are also formally identified through a specific assessment administration or other criteria, such as a teacher recommendation. When a student is formally identified into one of these three groups, he or she may attain mastery of any level on the proficiency scale, despite the provision of accommodations or modifications during the learning opportunity. In fact, it is the responsibility of the educational institution to ensure that exceptional students receive these allowable supports.

Accommodations Versus Modifications

In order for teachers to use proficiency scales appropriately with exceptional learners, it is paramount that they understand both accommodations and modifications. In *A School Leader's Guide to Standards-Based Grading*, the authors presented the following information about accommodations:

> Accommodations are changes to how information is presented, how students are asked to respond, where instruction takes place, and the time or scheduling of instruction. Accommodations do not change the level of proficiency. Students who receive accommodations are still expected to achieve the same levels of proficiency as students without accommodations. Accommodations simply allow students to demonstrate their learning in the ways that work best for them. (Heflebower et al., 2014, p. 72)

Based on this description, one might argue that accommodations *may* be provided for any learner, as the level of expectation for learning remains the same. This is true; however, for an exceptional learner, the word *may* changes to *must*. In other words, providing accommodations is not optional for students who have been formally identified as students with disabilities, English learners, or gifted and talented students.

Modifications, in contrast to accommodations, *do* change the level of learning expected of students. For students with disabilities or English learners, examples of common modifications include reducing the difficulty or amount of content, administering an assessment from a lower grade level, or changing the format of assessment items.

For gifted and talented students, modifications would involve raising the difficulty of content and assessments. Modifications typically only apply to a small number of students.

It is also important to remember that while the accommodations and modifications in a student's IEP are specific to the individual learner, they are not typically specific to a particular standard or learning target. In order to provide better support to an individual learner on proficiency scales, it is often worthwhile to identify accommodations or modifications specific to the learning targets on each scale. These accommodations and modifications are *in addition to* those listed in a student's individual learning plan and may be used when content on the proficiency scale is being taught. Since they are administered during the opportunity to learn, it is appropriate to consider them instructional supports. If they do not change the grade-level expectation, they can be called instructional accommodations. If they do change the grade-level expectation, it is appropriate to call them modifications.

Consider the proficiency scale for second-grade mathematics in figure 6.1, which also appeared in chapter 2 (page 20). Possible instructional accommodations and modifications specific to this proficiency scale are displayed in table 6.1 (page 78). The intention is for these additional instructional supports to better support the student while learning the content on the proficiency scale. When teachers determine and implement instructional accommodations or modifications specific to a proficiency scale, the likelihood for student success on the scale increases. This is especially true when these supports are provided in addition to the general adjustments already listed on a student's individual learning plan.

In the following sections, we explore the details of instructional accommodations and modifications, as well as how to develop them based on proficiency scales.

Strand: Measurement **Topic:** Word Problems With Money **Grade:** 2			
Score 4.0	In addition to score 3.0, in-depth inferences and applications that go beyond what was taught, such as: • Write, solve, and share a multi-step word problem involving dollar bills, quarters, dimes, nickels, and pennies • The student will count back change for values up to $10.00		**Sample Activities**
	3.5	In addition to score 3.0 performance, in-depth inferences and applications with partial success	
Score 3.0	The student will: • Solve word problems involving dollar bills, quarters, dimes, nickels, and pennies The student exhibits no major errors or omissions.		**Shopping activity:** **Materials for each pair**: word problems involving buying things, coins, dollar bills, white boards, markers, erasers **Procedures:** Students work with a partner. One partner is the buyer, and the other partner is the seller. The buyer draws a card, reads the problem, and solves it on the white board, using the money if needed to solve the problem. The seller checks the answer to be sure it is correct. The partners switch roles and play again. They continue playing, taking turns as the buyer and the seller.
	2.5	No major errors or omissions regarding 2.0 content and partial knowledge of the 3.0 content	

Score 2.0	There are no major errors or omissions regarding the simpler details and processes as the student:
	• Recognizes or recalls specific terminology, such as:
	  · *all together*, *coin*, *decimal*, *remaining*, *value*
	• Performs basic processes, such as:
	  · Identify coin values (quarter, dime, nickel, penny)
	  · Use $ and ¢ symbols appropriately
	  · Add or subtract different coins to determine a total amount of money or money remaining
	However, the student exhibits major errors or omissions regarding the more complex ideas and processes.
			Students match pictures of coins with cards displaying values (picture of quarter = $.25 or 25¢).

	1.5	Partial knowledge of the 2.0 content, but major errors or omissions regarding the 3.0 content	
Score 1.0	With help, a partial understanding of some of the simpler details and processes and some of the more complex ideas and processes		
	0.5	With help, a partial understanding of the 2.0 content, but not the 3.0 content	
Score 0.0	Even with help, no understanding or skill demonstrated		

Source: Adapted from Marzano et al., 2013, p. 264.

Figure 6.1: Proficiency scale and sample activities for word problems with money.

Table 6.1: Sample Accommodations and Modifications for Word Problems With Money

Accommodations	Modifications
The student is paired with a para-educator or the teacher in order to participate in the shopping activity.	The student is provided a performance task that requires that he or she follows a budget for purchasing items for a family camping trip.
The student is provided a graphic organizer for creating and solving a word problem.	The student is provided word problems involving dimes, nickels, and pennies, and the word problems are read to the student, as needed.
The student is provided word problems that are in his or her native language.	The student is provided simple one-step word problems involving dimes, nickels, and pennies in his or her native language.

Accommodating Students' Needs

When identifying the most appropriate instructional supports for individual proficiency scales, first and foremost, these supports should align to a specific learning target or a cluster of learning targets on the scale. For example, consider a learning target that reads, "The learner will describe the difference between mass and weight." An appropriate instructional support might be to provide sentence prompts for describing the difference between mass and weight. This accommodation is specifically designed for that particular learning target. Teachers might also consider listing multiple supports, if possible, to give options as the content is being taught. In order to plan appropriate accommodations for a specific proficiency scale, teachers can follow a four-step process.

1. Examine the individual student plan to identify allowable accommodations.

2. Select the most appropriate general accommodations from the plan to ensure the student can access the content on the proficiency scale. Then, identify additional instructional accommodations specific to the content at each level of the proficiency scale (score 2.0, score 3.0, and score 4.0).

3. Be sure to maintain the grade-level learning expectation (score 3.0).

4. Document the instructional accommodations by listing them on the student's proficiency scale.

The proficiency scale in figure 6.2 is an example of a product that might evolve as a result of these four steps. The general education scale is the foundation, and the accommodations appear on the right side of the scale. These instructional supports are simply ideas for the teacher to implement when circumstances call for them. It is important to reiterate that accommodations do not change the level of learning required by the standard, they simply support the student in acquiring and demonstrating the knowledge or skill.

The following vignette showcases a student with a disability and how his teacher provides support through the use of accommodations specific to a proficiency scale.

Miss Schultz is a seventh-grade math teacher who has worked diligently to develop proficiency scales for all of her priority standards. Currently, she is working to support students on the standard related to angles of triangles. Jacob, a seventh-grade student, was identified as an exceptional learner in kindergarten; therefore, as a result of his learning disability he has an individualized education plan (IEP). Jacob's IEP allows for accommodations which Miss Schultz understands clearly. Accommodations allow for her to provide appropriate supports for Jacob, but she can't decrease the requirements of the standards for grade 7 mathematics. Jacob, like all of her seventh

continued ⇨

	Proficiency Scale	Instructional Accommodations
4.0	In addition to score 3.0 performance, the student demonstrates in-depth inferences and applications that go beyond what was taught. For example, the student will: • Create a real-world word problem, and model it with an equation with a letter or symbol to represent the unknown. Solve the equation, explaining the strategy or strategies used in the process.	The student will be provided the following supports, as needed: • Presentation of one part of the task to the student at a time, allowing for completion of the part before the next is presented
3.5	In addition to score 3.0, in-depth inferences and applications with partial success	
3.0	The student will: • Solve two-step word problems using the four operations • Represent two-step word problems using equations with a letter standing for the unknown quantity • Assess the reasonableness of answers using mental computation and estimation strategies including rounding The student exhibits no major errors or omissions.	The student will be provided the following supports, as needed: • A graphic organizer for solving two-step word problems • Worked examples to follow when representing two-step word problems using equations with a letter standing for the unknown quantity • Probing questions and feedback when assessing the reasonableness of answers • Support when reading word problems independently
2.5	No major errors or omissions regarding 2.0 content and partial knowledge of the 3.0 content	
2.0	There are no major errors or omissions regarding the simpler details and processes. The student will recognize or recall specific vocabulary, such as: • *unknown, known, equations, estimation, rounding, reasonableness, mental computation, represent, variable* The student will perform basic processes, such as: • Solve one-step word problems using the four operations However, the student exhibits major errors or omissions regarding the more complex ideas and processes.	The student will be provided the following supports, as needed: • Word cards for recalling specific vocabulary terms and their definitions • A graphic organizer for solving one-step word problems • Support when reading word problems independently
1.5	Partial knowledge of the 2.0 content but major errors or omissions regarding the 3.0 content	
1.0	With help, a partial understanding of some 2.0 content (the simpler details and processes) and some 3.0 content (the more complex ideas and processes)	
0.5	With help, a partial understanding of the 2.0 content but not the 3.0 content	
0.0	Even with help, no understanding or skill demonstrated	

Source: Adapted from Marzano et al., 2013, p. 220.

Figure 6.2: A mathematics scale with accommodations for students with disabilities.

graders, must attain mastery of target content (score 3.0) on all proficiency scales, including the scale for angles of triangles.

Jacob's IEP lists typical accommodations, such as extended time, providing a quiet work space, and having directions read out loud. However, Miss Schultz has determined it necessary to provide supports beyond those listed in Jacob's IEP. She has taken time to also identify accommodations that are specific to each proficiency scale that she teaches. For example, score 3.0 on the angles of triangles proficiency scale states: "I can use evidence to informally explain relationships among the angles of triangles, including the sum of interior angles and angle-angle similarity." An instructional support she determined as appropriate and allowable for Jacob is to provide worked examples for him to examine as he completes items and tasks related to this level on the proficiency scale. Providing worked examples does not change the level of expectation but does provide support to Jacob. Miss Schultz identified other accommodations for score 3.0 and score 2.0, as well. Miss Schultz and Jacob share the common goal of score 3.0 mastery, and the accommodations she implements during the opportunity to learn will increase the likelihood that he will meet this goal.

Modifying the Proficiency Scale

There are also students whose individual learning plans require modifications, or changes to the expected level of learning. Once again, a series of steps guide teachers to develop appropriate modifications for a specific proficiency scale.

1. Examine the individual student plan to identify allowable modifications.

2. Select the most appropriate modifications from the plan to ensure that the student is able to access the content on the proficiency scale. Then, identify additional modifications specific to each level on the proficiency scale.

3. The scale-specific modifications will decrease or increase the difficulty of the learning target, dependent upon the exceptional learner category.

4. List the appropriate modifications on the student's proficiency scale.

The proficiency scale in figure 6.3 includes possible modifications for a student related to the word problems with money proficiency scale. It is important to note that the modifications decrease the level of expectation.

The degree to which the teacher needs to modify the general education proficiency scale is dependent on the learner requiring the modifications. The following questions can help determine how significantly we should modify the content and learning expectations.

- Is the most appropriate modification to move the content up or down on the scale (for example, score 2.0 to 3.0, score 4.0 to 3.0)?

- Is the most appropriate modification to substitute a related proficiency scale from a lower or higher grade level?

- Is the most appropriate modification to customize the levels on the proficiency scale for the individual student?

We explore each of these options in the following sections.

Moving Content Up or Down the Scale

When the teacher determines that it is most appropriate to adjust the content levels within the scale, the result is a subtle modification, as language simply moves up or down a level on the proficiency scale. For example, consider the proficiency scale regarding word problems with money presented earlier in this chapter (page 77). Figure 6.4 (page 82) compares three versions of the learning targets for this scale: (1) the general education proficiency

Prioritized Standard: Solve two-step word problems using the four operations. Represent these problems using equations with a letter standing for the unknown quantity. Assess the reasonableness of answers using mental computation and estimation strategies including rounding. Operations and Algebraic Thinking—Solve problems involving the four operations and identify and explain patterns in arithmetic.

	Proficiency Scale	Modifications
4.0	In addition to score 3.0 performance, the student demonstrates in-depth inferences and applications that go beyond what was taught. For example, the student will: • Create a real-world word problem, and model it with an equation with a letter or symbol to represent the unknown. Solve the equation, explaining the strategy or strategies used in the process.	The student will: • Solve two-step word problems using addition and subtraction • Represent one-step word problems using equations with a letter standing for the unknown quantity • Assess the reasonableness of answers from options provided
3.5	In addition to score 3.0, in-depth inferences and applications with partial success	
3.0	The student will: • Solve two-step word problems using the four operations • Represent two-step word problems using equations with a letter standing for the unknown quantity • Assess the reasonableness of answers using mental computation and estimation strategies including rounding The student exhibits no major errors or omissions.	The student will: • Solve one-step word problems using addition and subtraction
2.5	No major errors or omissions regarding 2.0 content and partial knowledge of the 3.0 content	
2.0	There are no major errors or omissions regarding the simpler details and processes. The student will recognize or recall specific vocabulary, such as: • *unknown, known, equations, estimation, rounding, reasonableness, mental computation, represent, variable* The student will perform basic processes, such as: • Solve one-step word problems using the four operations However, the student exhibits major errors or omissions regarding the more complex ideas and processes.	The student will: • Match specific vocabulary terms and provided definitions related to solving two-step word problems • Identify the steps in solving one-step word problems using addition and subtraction
1.5	Partial knowledge of the 2.0 content but major errors or omissions regarding the 3.0 content	
1.0	With help, a partial understanding of some 2.0 content (the simpler details and processes) and some 3.0 content (the more complex ideas and processes)	
0.5	With help, a partial understanding of the 2.0 content but not the 3.0 content	
0.0	Even with help, no understanding or skill demonstrated	

Source: Adapted from Marzano et al., 2013, p. 220.

Figure 6.3: A mathematics scale with modifications for students with disabilities.

scale, (2) a modified scale with decreased expectations, and (3) a modified scale with increased expectations. The modified versions simply move the existing content either up or down on the proficiency scale. When increasing expectations, the teacher will need to create new content for score 4.0.

Substituting a Scale From a Different Grade Level

This method involves a higher degree of modification—identifying a completely different (but related) proficiency scale to use with the learner.

This method of modification works particularly well in English language arts, as there is often a related proficiency scale at a higher or a lower grade level. Consider a sixth-grade student who is formally identified as gifted and talented. The team of teachers who support this learner knows that the grade 6 proficiency scale for theme and central idea is not appropriate for the learner. Therefore, they examine the seventh-grade scale for the same topic. Finally, they determine that the eighth-grade scale for theme and central idea is the most appropriate scale for this student. In order to make this

	General Education Scale	Decreased Expectations	Increased Expectations
Score 4.0	The student will: • Write, solve, and share a multi-step word problem involving dollar bills, quarters, dimes, nickels, and pennies	The student will: • Solve word problems involving dollar bills, quarters, dimes, nickels, and pennies	The student will: • Use mental computation and estimation strategies to assess the reasonableness of an answer at different stages of solving a multi-step word problem involving money • Design scenarios in which solving word problems with money is an essential skill
Score 3.0	The student will: • Solve word problems involving dollar bills, quarters, dimes, nickels, and pennies	The student will: • Identify coin values (quarter, dime, nickel, penny) • Add or subtract different coins to determine a total amount of money or money remaining	The student will: • Write, solve, and share a multi-step word problem involving dollar bills, quarters, dimes, nickels, and pennies
Score 2.0	The student will: • Recognize or recall specific terminology, such as: *$, ¢, value, coin, penny, nickel, dime, quarter, dollar, all together, remaining, decimal* • Use $ and ¢ symbols appropriately • Identify coin values (quarter, dime, nickel, penny) • Add or subtract different coins to determine a total amount of money or money remaining	The student will: • Recognize or recall specific terminology, such as: *$, ¢, value, coin, penny, nickel, dime, quarter, dollar, all together, remaining, decimal* • Use $ and ¢ symbols appropriately	The student will: • Solve word problems involving dollar bills, quarters, dimes, nickels, and pennies

Source: © 2019 by Fulton County Schools. Used with permission.

Figure 6.4: Moving content up or down the scale.

decision, the teacher team considers which scale will challenge the learner, but not so much that it is too far beyond the student's level of ability. Clearly, the level of expectation has increased by choosing the grade 8 scale, which is allowable because of the formal identification of the student as gifted and talented. This same process for modifying a proficiency scale can be used for a student with a disability or an English learner. However, the scale determined to be the most appropriate would be from a lower grade level.

Customizing Scale Levels for an Individual Student

There are times when the best approach to modifying a proficiency scale is to customize the scale for a specific learner. Customization, in this case, means determining a learning target that relates to the prioritized standard, but also aligns to the individual student's ability level. This customization requires that the teacher or team of teachers who support the learner know him or her well. It also requires that the educators involved in the customization process

understand the content well enough to include appropriate learning targets on the scale.

For example, consider a third-grade student who has been identified as gifted and talented. The class is working on a proficiency scale for the standard, "The student will describe early American Indian cultures and their development in North America." The teacher has determined that the third-grade proficiency scale needs modification, but there is not a scale at a higher grade level related to this same content. The teacher customizes the proficiency scale to meet the individual needs of this learner, which in this case, involves customization at score 4.0 only since the student needs opportunities for learning beyond grade level. The scale in figure 6.5 shows the teacher's modifications.

In the case of this social studies scale, the gifted and talented student may participate in some or even most of the learning opportunities provided for all students. However, when the teacher deems it appropriate, the student will engage in the modified content. This will occur when the teacher is

GRADE 3 SOCIAL STUDIES		
Prioritized Standard: Describe early American Indian cultures and their development in North America.		
	Proficiency Scale	**Modified Proficiency Scale**
4.0	• Gather, analyze, and organize information from multiple sources on American Indians. Then compare and contrast to other groups (such as Native Americans versus European colonists).	• Make a claim about how contributions made by American Indians have impacted his or her life. Communicate in a self-selected manner regarding whether the impact is positive or negative. Provide evidence to support the claim and give reasoning as to why the impact is positive or negative.
3.0	• Explain how and why the contributions made by American Indians are still being used today.	
2.0	• Identify the regions in which American Indians settled (Arctic, Northwest, Southwest, Plains, Northeast, and Southeast). • Describe how American Indian groups used their environment to obtain food, clothing, and shelter. • Compare and contrast how American Indian groups used their environments to obtain food, clothing, and shelter.	

Source: © 2019 by Fulton County Schools. Used with permission.

Figure 6.5: A social studies scale with modifications for gifted and talented students.

confident that the student has acquired the knowledge and skill on the grade-level proficiency scale and is therefore ready for a learning opportunity that requires an even higher level of cognition. Additionally, this particular modification requires a high level of independence, which is often the case with modifications for gifted and talented students. In this scenario, expectations can and should be greater than for the general education students in the classroom.

There will likely be times when customization is needed for a student who is working below grade level. This may translate to a scale that looks very little like the grade-level proficiency scale in that every level on the scale is customized for the learner. However, because it aligns to the student's ability level, it is appropriate.

Visit **MarzanoResources.com/reproducibles** to download a free reproducible worksheet that summarizes the information for determining appropriate accommodations or modifications.

Special Considerations for English Learners

English learners (ELs) are students who need support in an educational environment as a result of having limited English proficiency. In fact, some students in this category of exceptional learners have heard very little English prior to entering school, regardless of age. As a result, the academic content in proficiency scales will have very little relevance to some English learners until they have developed sufficient English language skills.

In order to support students in acquiring adequate use of the English language, multiple organizations have identified and described levels of English language acquisition. The World-Class Instructional Design and Assessment (WIDA) Consortium is one such organization that supports more than forty U.S. states, territories, and federal agencies dedicated to supporting English learners in K–12 contexts (Board of Regents of the University of Wisconsin

System, 2018). Besides developing English language proficiency standards, WIDA has defined six language acquisition levels that rate students' use of both social and academic language. Figure 6.6 displays these levels.

Per the descriptors associated with each level of language acquisition, learners at the lower levels have very limited use of both social and academic language, if any. As a result, these students will need significant support in acquiring the ability to participate in the educational opportunities offered. This support often comes in the form of specific English language instruction, which sometimes takes place outside of the general education classroom. In essence, for students who have limited use of the English language, learning the subject-specific content on proficiency scales is secondary to gaining stronger use of the English language.

As a result of these challenges, a first step in supporting English learners is to make a decision about the degree of language acquisition necessary for students to engage with the content on the proficiency scales with some degree of success. In other

1	**Entering**—Knows and uses minimal social language and minimal academic language with visual and graphic support
2	**Beginning**—Knows and uses some social English and general academic language with visual and graphic support
3	**Developing**—Knows and uses social English and some specific academic language with visual and graphic support
4	**Expanding**—Knows and uses social English and some technical academic language
5	**Bridging**—Knows and uses social English and academic language when working with grade-level materials
6	**Reaching**—Knows and uses social and academic language at the highest level measured by the test

Source: Adapted from Gottlieb, Cranley, & Oliver, 2007, p. 45.

Figure 6.6: Levels of language acquisition.

words, educators must answer the question, When should the proficiency scales become the primary focus in students' daily experience as learners? This is typically a school-level decision, or it may even be a district decision for all schools within the system. While there is no universal rule for which language-acquisition level is adequate for engaging students in grade-level proficiency scales, schools commonly set level 3 (developing) or level 4 (expanding) as the benchmark for this purpose.

Imagine a student who is at level 2 (beginning). This means that he or she knows and uses some social English and general academic language, but only with visual and graphic support. When language use is this limited, the student and the teacher are both likely to experience high levels of frustration in relation to showing growth on a proficiency scale. For this reason, it may prove beneficial to delay focusing on mastery of score 3.0 on proficiency scales until the student develops adequate understanding and use of the English language. During the time that English learners are focused on building their English language skills, instructional accommodations or modifications may be appropriate. Once a student has command of the English language, his or her teachers can gradually minimize and perhaps eventually eliminate the use of these supports.

Communication About Performance

Regardless of which group of exceptional learners (students with disabilities, gifted and talented students, or English learners) a student falls into, it is important that adequate and appropriate communication occur between the school and the student's parents or guardians. There is a variety of methods for ensuring that parents are aware of the fact that the student received accommodations or modifications while participating in learning opportunities. Without this information, parents may misunderstand the student's current level of learning. For example, consider a student with a disability who receives accommodations and attains a score 3.0 on

the standard. Without knowledge of the accommodations, the parent may mistakenly believe the student is independently performing at grade level.

The progress report in figure 6.7 is an example of how one school ensures parents are aware of accommodations and modifications provided to their students. Each topic on the progress report would have an associated proficiency scale; the score represents this student's current level of knowledge on that scale.

Third Quarter Progress Report Adalyn Montgomery Grade 2			
ELA	**Score**	**Mathematics**	**Score**
Main Idea and Supporting Detail	2.5	Addition and Subtraction	2.0
Story Elements	2.0	Arrays	1.5
Comparing Two Texts	2.0	Money	2.0
Narrative Writing	2.0	Geometry	2.5
Collaborative Conversations	2.5		

Teacher Comments:

Adalyn is having a very positive third quarter. She is working diligently to learn the content of the topics that are currently being addressed. Her proficiency scale scores are to be celebrated, as they demonstrate that knowledge and skill have been acquired for the important topics that we are studying. Please note that the allowable accommodations are being administered as necessary throughout this nine-week period. Some of those accommodations include: providing graphic organizers, repeating information, rephrasing directions or information, providing manipulatives, and others. Thank you for the support provided to your daughter in the home environment. She is making progress, and we will work hard through the remainder of the year to improve Adalyn's level of mastery on the priority topics.

Figure 6.7: Communicating about accommodations.

While it clearly requires time on the part of the teacher to provide this level of communication, it proves valuable in ensuring that everyone involved has adequate understanding of the student's level of performance and the supports provided in order to attain current levels of mastery. Obviously, there is no single correct way to communicate with parents and guardians. In addition to the progress report, a teacher may choose to communicate such information during a face-to-face conference with a parent or guardian, in an email or phone conversation, or even through anecdotal information made available to parents in the gradebook platform. Teachers, teacher teams, and schools must commit to determining the method that works best for them relative to providing important and accurate information about learning for their students and families.

Summary

This chapter provides information about how to determine accommodations and modifications for students with disabilities, English learners, and gifted and talented students. Accommodations provide help to learners but do not change the content or expectations, while modifications do adjust the learning target. Exceptional learners often have individual learning plans, which list appropriate accommodations or modifications that teachers must provide during learning opportunities. Sometimes these are not aligned to the specific skills on a proficiency scale; therefore, it is often helpful to determine additional instructional supports specific to learning targets on a scale. These instructional accommodations or modifications help exceptional learners access the grade-level content as they participate in classroom learning experiences. Teachers of English learners must particularly consider whether it is most appropriate for the student to focus on academic content or language acquisition. Finally, accurate and meaningful communication between the school and parents is paramount. The next chapter is all about developing and using scales for nonacademic behaviors and skills.

Chapter 6 Comprehension Questions

1. What groups of students are considered exceptional learners?

2. What is the difference between accommodations and modifications?

3. What is important to remember regarding using proficiency scales when a student requires accommodations? Modifications?

4. What should teachers remember about English learners who have limited understanding of the English language? Why is this important?

5. Why is it important for teachers to communicate with parents of exceptional learners?

CHAPTER 7

Scales for Behaviors That Promote Academic Success

Proficiency scales are most often associated with academic content. However, it is also important to provide feedback to learners on nonacademic factors that promote academic success. Examples of nonacademic factors include submitting work on time, participating in classroom opportunities, following classroom rules, and getting along with peers. These nonacademic factors and others are essential to students' success in school and in life.

The Rationale for Nonacademic Scales

The practice of giving students feedback on behaviors—such as submitting work on time, coming prepared for class, and following classroom expectations—is not uncommon. In 2006, Marzano wrote about this in *Classroom Assessment and Grading That Work*. He stated that "a number of studies and reports over the last few decades have noted the importance of 'life skills'—information and skills that are not specific to traditional academic subject areas but are important to success in a variety of situations" (p. 25). He also shared numerous studies that attest to the importance of

behaviors such as effort, working well in groups, adhering to rules, showing respect for others, and being punctual (Marzano, 2006).

Despite information such as this being available to teachers, it is not unusual for teachers to merge academic performance with behaviors. According to Thomas R. Guskey (2011), grading expert, this is a ludicrous practice.

> If someone proposed combining measures of height, weight, diet, and exercise into a single number or mark to represent a person's physical condition, we would consider it laughable. How could the combination of such diverse measures yield anything meaningful? Yet every day, teachers combine aspects of students' achievement, attitude, responsibility, effort, and behavior into a single grade that's recorded on a report card—and no one questions it. (p. 21)

Combining academic and behavioral factors into one grade misrepresents what students know and are able to do. If a student receives an omnibus grade of 70 percent, it might indicate that the student demonstrated understanding of 70 percent of the required content, or it could mean that the student met all the standards but frequently talked out of turn and to classmates during instruction, which negatively impacted the scores earned. Practices such as this result in a significant problem when it comes to providing clear and accurate feedback to students.

To further illustrate the problem, consider a teacher who assigns an end-of-unit project related to numerous academic standards. After presenting the details related to the project, the teacher communicates the due date for submission of the project and informs students that ten points will be deducted from the total score earned for each day the project is submitted late. Obviously, this practice impacts the accuracy of feedback provided to a learner who submits a near-perfect project four days late. As a result of the late submission, the grade assigned to this piece of student work is not a reflection of its quality. For this reason, separate scales that provide feedback to students on behaviors that promote academic success are essential in a standards-based learning environment.

One error in thinking often associated with using nonacademic scales is the idea that the nonacademic skills become less important because students do not see consequences to their academic grades when they turn in work late or disengage from class. In actuality, the opposite is true. When a teacher or team of teachers showcases desired nonacademic skills with proficiency scales, it provides increased clarity regarding desired behaviors. Nonacademic scales are also tools for giving precise feedback to a learner or group of learners. Students receive feedback and scores on nonacademic factors separate from academic scores, which makes both types of feedback more accurate and meaningful.

As an example of a scale for a behavior that promotes academic success, consider the grade 4 proficiency scale for work habits in figure 7.1. This scale communicates the work habits that are important in this fourth-grade classroom. With such a scale, all learners can clearly understand the specific work

Work Habits	
Grade 4	
Score 4.0	The student: Self-monitors and corrects behavior that doesn't meet score 3.0 expectations Explains why score 3.0 work habits are necessary for learning
3.5	In addition to score 3.0 performance, in-depth applications with partial success
Score 3.0	The student: Demonstrates work habits necessary for learning, including— • Being on task, completing tasks, being prepared • Using time appropriately • Persisting through a difficult task • Managing property (personal and school supplies, technology) • Organizing their personal and classroom materials
2.5	In addition to score 3.0 performance, in-depth applications with partial success
Score 2.0	The student: Describes work habits necessary for learning
1.5	Partial success of the 2.0 content but major errors or omissions regarding the 3.0 content
Score 1.0	With help, partial success of some of the simpler details and processes and some of the more complex ideas and processes

Source: © 2019 by Columbia Public Schools. Used with permission.

Figure 7.1: Sample nonacademic scale for work habits.

habits they must demonstrate. When one or more of the work habits is absent, a teacher can initiate a meaningful conversation with a learner about what he or she has observed and what the student can do differently in the future. In the case of this scale, work habits are a primary instructional focus just as main idea or place value are a primary focus in relation to academic scales.

A Process for Developing Nonacademic Scales

In order to develop a scale that provides feedback on nonacademic attributes, a teacher or team of teachers should enact the following four steps.

1. Brainstorm a list of nonacademic factors that are important to foster in students.

2. Determine which three to five attributes are most important to develop into learning progressions.

3. Write a proficiency scale or a rubric to articulate a learning progression for each attribute.

4. Use the scales to give feedback to learners about their current level of performance on nonacademic factors.

Brainstorm Important Behaviors

There are many nonacademic behaviors that are associated with learning. Some of the most common include turning work in on time, following classroom rules, coming prepared for class, and cooperating with others in the classroom. Historically, it has been common practice for an individual teacher to identify which nonacademic behaviors are important to emphasize in their own classroom. However, in a standards-based learning environment, it is best for a team of teachers to identify the most important nonacademic behaviors so that students receive consistent instruction and feedback on these skills alongside the academic content identified for a grade level or course. Therefore, it is paramount that teachers or teacher teams take adequate time to brainstorm a list of the factors they consider critical for all students. Figure

7.2 shows an example of what might result from a brainstorming session for nonacademic factors.

Select Three to Five Essential Attributes

After generating a list of potential nonacademic factors, it is time to select the most important three to five skills to develop into a learning progression. If an individual teacher is making this decision, he or she can consider the attributes that require the most instructional attention for scale development. To illustrate, consider a kindergarten classroom where students are just learning how to get along and work with other students. The teacher's thought process may sound like this:

These young learners need clarity about how to get along with other students because the classroom is a new environment for most of them. Also, I spend a lot of time providing direction about this over the course of an academic year. I am going to develop a proficiency scale for this important nonacademic skill.

MIDDLE SCHOOL NONACADEMIC FACTOR BRAINSTORMING LIST

Works cooperatively with others
Follows directions
Uses time wisely
Completes work on time
Works independently
Follows classroom routines and procedures
Demonstrates self-control
Respects property of self, others, and school
Turns in all work on time
Exercises listening skills
Gets along with peers
Demonstrates self-initiative
Participates in classroom activities
Demonstrates self-advocacy skills
Puts forth effort

Figure 7.2: Sample brainstorming list.

If a team of teachers is deciding on the most important nonacademic factors, they can use a consensus-building process to ensure that the majority of the team agrees on which factors are selected as the most important. Prior to making decisions about the nonacademic factors, the team determines the required degree of agreement in order for a factor to be selected as a priority. This might just mean that a majority of team members selects the attribute or it could be a specific percentage (for example, 75 percent of team members). During the process, team members can discuss individual factors to build consensus.

The following vignette describes one such process implemented by a district made up of many schools.

Madison County Schools has worked diligently to identify priority standards and write proficiency scales for all academic areas over the course of the past four years. Additionally, they decided that it is important for nonacademic factors to be articulated into learning progressions. Since Madison County is a very large district, they initially sent out a survey to gather input from educators across the district regarding which nonacademic factors are the most important. Once they received the survey results, district leaders discerned approximately twenty nonacademic behaviors for consideration.

In order to create proficiency scales for nonacademic factors that are grade-level appropriate, Madison County decided to create proficiency scales for nonacademic factors for the following grade bands: preK through second grade, third through fifth grades, sixth through eighth grades, and high school. Educators representing each grade band came together for a day to determine which factors from the overall list would be developed into proficiency scales. In order to select the nonacademic factors, educators first worked individually to

rank the list for their grade band. Following the individual work time, they formed small groups within each grade band. Participants in each group compared their rankings and came to agreement about the top four nonacademic factors. Finally, the entire grade band came together and replicated the process completed in the smaller groups. This process resulted in three to five nonacademic factors for each grade band.

The identified factors varied slightly by grade band, but for grades 6 through 8, the list included: work completion, class preparedness, collaboration, and self-management. Once the factors were agreed upon, teams of educators developed proficiency scales.

Write a Scale or Rubric for Each Nonacademic Factor

Teachers can write scales for nonacademic factors in the same manner as academic proficiency scales. They address score 3.0—the target content—first. This target content is the expectation for all learners. Once score 3.0 is complete, they determine simpler score 2.0 content. Just as with an academic proficiency scale, this simple content often includes vocabulary and prerequisite knowledge or skill. Score 4.0 is the complex content level and communicates a performance that is beyond the target expectation. Therefore, learners are not required to attain mastery of this level. However, because these scales display learning progressions for nonacademic content, it may be that a greater number of students have the potential to attain a score of 4.0. Finally, score 1.0 represents students who require help in order to demonstrate what they know or are able to do. This may include reminders, prompts, cues, and other forms of support. While not essential, it may be helpful to include half-point increments on the nonacademic scales. This may be especially true for the sake of consistency if half-points are included on the academic scales.

Figure 7.3 is an example that displays a learning progression for one nonacademic factor—following classroom rules. The format is the same as that used for many academic proficiency scales. The scale in figure 7.4 (page 94) is an example of what educators might collaboratively develop for the nonacademic factor of work completion for grades 6 through 8. The format is rubric-like, rather than that of a typical academic proficiency scale, which is an acceptable format for articulating a learning progression. Scale developers can decide which format best serves their purposes. This rubric includes information about degree of frequency, which requires a teacher to keep track of infractions in order to determine an appropriate score level. However, it is a necessary component for ensuring that all teachers in the school or district score students consistently.

A final important idea regarding developing nonacademic proficiency scales is that there is no one right way to complete this task nor one correct format for nonacademic scales. For example, figure 7.5 (page 94) displays a list of critical nonacademic skills determined by a team of second- and third-grade teachers and the scale to be used for giving student feedback. This scale looks different than either of the two previous examples provided. The format of the scale should meet the needs of the users of the scale.

Use Scales to Give Feedback to Learners

Just as academic proficiency scales provide meaningful feedback to learners about their current level of performance on important academic content, these nonacademic scales can do the same for performance on behavioral factors. A teacher can periodically record performance on any of the nonacademic skills in order to determine an overall score at certain points during an academic year (for example, mid-quarter, end of quarter, end of semester), similar to an academic report card.

FOLLOWING CLASSROOM RULES	
Score 4.0	In addition to score 3.0 performance, the student demonstrates in-depth inferences and applications that go beyond what was taught. • For example, explains potential problems if classroom rules are not followed • For example, self-corrects behavior that isn't in compliance with a classroom rule
Score 3.0	The student: • Follows classroom rules determined by the collective efforts of the teacher and the class • Listens and follows verbal directions • Corrects behavior when redirected by the teacher
Score 2.0	The student recognizes or recalls specific vocabulary, such as: • *redirected, verbal directions* The student performs basic processes, such as: • States classroom rules determined by the collective efforts of the teacher and the class • Repeats verbal directions when asked
Score 1.0	With help, the student demonstrates partial success at score 2.0 and score 3.0.
Score 0.0	Even with help, the student demonstrates no understanding of the 2.0 and score 3.0 content.

Figure 7.3: Sample proficiency scale for following classroom rules.

The example recording sheet in figure 7.6 (page 95) includes the same skills as figure 7.5, as a teacher would use the two forms in conjunction. Additionally, the teacher can offer feedback to a learner regarding how to improve his or her performance. The teacher can also share this information with parents.

Work Completion				
	Score 4.0 **Consistently Exceeds Expectations**	**Score 3.0** **Consistently Meets Expectations**	**Score 2.0** **Inconsistently Meets Expectations**	**Score 1.0** **Does Not Meet Expectations**
Completes work and turns it in punctually	Is punctual or early turning in assignments	Is punctual in turning in assignments	Is not always punctual in turning in assignments	Is not punctual in turning in assignments
Degree of frequency	No infractions	0–2 infractions	3–5 infractions	More than 5 infractions

Figure 7.4: Rubric for work completion.

Success-Ready Skills, Grades 2–3			
Work Habits	**Interactions With Peers**	**Interactions With Adults**	**Personal Growth**
Demonstrates work habits necessary for learning Identifies and performs processes, such as: Stays on task, completing tasks Uses time appropriately Works with effort Follows directions Persists through a difficult task (productive struggle, emotional regulation: identifying and expressing feelings) Manages property (personal and school supplies and technology) Organizes his or her personal and classroom materials	Utilizes communication and social skills to interact effectively with peers Identifies and performs processes, such as: Recognizes and applies examples of behaviors, community norms, and how the behaviors affect others Works and plays cooperatively with peers Recognizes and applies the characteristics of good friends and positive community members Recognizes and applies accurate statements about, or examples of, appropriate and inappropriate social skills	Utilizes communication and social skills to interact effectively with adults Identifies and performs processes, such as: Cooperates with adults through words, tone, and action (responds appropriately to directions and redirects) Identifies and uses communication strategies Uses active listening Identifies and uses problem-solving tools (including asking for help, using your words, and so on)	Will identify, set, share, and monitor personal and learning goals for oneself Identifies and performs processes, such as: Demonstrates an awareness of strengths, interests, and growth areas that contribute to success in school Recognizes or recalls examples of personal strengths and interests (for example, physical behaviors or factors that are barriers, cooperation between teacher and student—based on feedback) Recognizes or recalls way to achieve goals Student can describe something one does well and with difficulty Shares goals

Scoring

  4 Excelling: Student goes above and beyond what was taught

  3 Proficient: Usually or almost always meets all parts of the learning goals

  2 Progressing: Meeting some parts of the goals; may need some support to meet the goals

  1 Emerging: Meets very few parts of the goals; needs support to meet parts of the goals

Figure 7.5: Example of nonacademic skills.

Success-Ready Skills	Scores					
	Week: ___	Week: ___	Week: ___	Week: ___	Week: ___	Week: ___
Work Habits						
Interactions With Adults						
Interactions With Peers						
Personal Growth						

Source: © 2019 by Columbia Public Schools. Used with permission.

Figure 7.6: Form for reporting nonacademic skills.

Proficiency scales for nonacademic factors ensure a more comprehensive understanding of student performance. For example, imagine a student who performs poorly on the majority of both the academic proficiency scales and the nonacademic scales. It seems likely that the academic performance may be at least in part because of the low performance on the nonacademic factors. This realization could result in a very meaningful conversation between the teacher and the student and will potentially lead to increased focus and improved performance on the nonacademic factors. As a result, the student's performance on both types of content goes up.

There is a variety of ways that students' academic and nonacademic skills can interact in the classroom. When scales for the nonacademic factors are in place, teachers often have a better idea of how to support learners. Consider table 7.1 (page 96), which displays possible teacher responses based on student performance for both academic and nonacademic factors. Clearly, the practice of separating academic and nonacademic factors provides the basis for impactful conversations between a teacher and his or her students. In the end, a performance of score 3.0 or higher on both academic and nonacademic factors is the goal.

Summary

This chapter discusses the importance of determining critical nonacademic factors that may impact academic performance in the classroom. It is important to separate these factors out from academic performance in order to ensure accurate and meaningful feedback for students. Teachers or teams should select three to five critical behavioral skills for which to develop scales. Students' performances on academic and nonacademic factors influence each other, and having clear metrics for both can offer teachers valuable insight as to how to best support learners.

Table 7.1: Options for Providing Feedback on Academic and Nonacademic Skills

Student Performance on Academic Proficiency Scales	Student Performance on Nonacademic Proficiency Scales	Possible Outcomes
Acceptable or Exceeding Expectations	Acceptable or Exceeding Expectations	• Teacher acknowledges student performance • Teacher encourages continued similar performance on both • Teacher may communicate with parents or guardians about student performance on both
Acceptable or Exceeding Expectations	Unacceptable or Below Expectations	• Teacher acknowledges student performance on academic factors • Teacher asks for student perspective on current nonacademic performance • Teacher provides additional insight on student's nonacademic performance and articulates expectations • Teacher encourages continued similar performance on academic factors • Teacher urges student to improve effort on nonacademic factors • Teacher may communicate with parents or guardians about student performance on both
Unacceptable or Below Expectations	Acceptable or Exceeding Expectations	• Teacher acknowledges student performance on nonacademic factors • Teacher asks for student perspective on current academic performance • Teacher provides additional insight into student's academic performance • Teacher encourages continued similar performance on nonacademic factors • Teacher provides ideas for how the student can receive additional support for improved performance on academic factors • Teacher may communicate with parents or guardians about student performance on both
Unacceptable or Below Expectations	Unacceptable or Below Expectations	• Teacher acknowledges positive student performance on academic and nonacademic factors • Teacher asks for student perspective on current performance • Teacher discusses the connection between nonacademic performance on academic performance • Teacher urges student to improve effort on nonacademic factor(s) • Teacher provides ideas for how the student can receive additional support for improved performance on academic factors • Teacher may communicate with parents or guardians about student performance on both

Chapter 7 Comprehension Questions

1. What are some common nonacademic factors that are viewed as important by most educators?

2. Why is it important to separate academic factors from nonacademic factors when giving feedback to learners?

3. How might performance on nonacademic factors be determined?

Epilogue

The intention of this book is to support any teacher, team of teachers, school, or district that is striving to improve student learning. It provides a method for achieving clarity about what students must know and be able to do, which is the first step in attaining this goal. While a positive impact on learning can indeed occur when an individual teacher implements scales, the degree of impact will undoubtedly be greater when more teachers participate in scale development and implementation. Regardless, completing the work related to proficiency scales is a process. As Heflebower and her colleagues (2014) stated, "Teachers need time to process with one another, try new ideas, receive feedback from peers, and—over time—change existing philosophies" (p. 113). This statement expresses the need for collaborative cultures and productive structures.

Scale implementation, while challenging, is doable if future users build understanding of the what, why, and how of proficiency scales. This book provides the pathway toward developing the necessary knowledge base. In chapter 1, we described a proficiency scale as a progression of knowledge, from simple to target to complex content. Chapter 2 provided various methods for developing proficiency scales. In chapter 3, we addressed one particular level on the scale in detail—score 4.0. Three categories of scale users were identified in chapter 4—teachers, students, and parents—along with ideas for use. The remaining chapters each addressed a topic related to proficiency scale implementation: using proficiency scales with rubrics and other tools (chapter 5), using scales with exceptional learners (chapter 6), and designing scales for nonacademic factors (chapter 7). Any teacher who aspires to become an expert on proficiency scales now has a complete resource for building the necessary expertise, especially because of the plethora of scale examples provided as a result of many generous contributions.

Proficiency scales fit within the broader initiative of standards-based learning. Teachers, leaders, and other educators who commit to standards-based learning propel their schools to higher levels of effectiveness. No doubt, it takes time, resources, and commitment. However, we are confident that the work around proficiency scales can and will have a positive impact in any classroom, school, or district.

APPENDIX A
Example Scales

Topic: ELA

Grade Level or Course: Kindergarten

Standard: With prompting and support, the student will identify characters, settings, and major events in a story.

Score 4.0: Complex Content Demonstrations of learning that go above and beyond what was explicitly taught The student will (for example): • Independently read an emergent-level text (DRA/BAS level 6/D or higher) and answer questions about the characters, settings, and events of the story
Score 3.0: Target Content The expectations for all students The student will: • Identify characters in a story • Identify setting in a story • Identify major events in a story
Score 2.0: Simple Content Foundational knowledge, simpler procedures, isolated details, vocabulary The student will recognize or recall specific vocabulary, such as: • *character*, *setting*, *event* The student will perform basic processes, such as: • Select a character in the story from a set of picture choices • Select a setting in the story from a set of picture choices • Identify one event in the story
Score 1.0: With help, the student can perform score 2.0 and 3.0 expectations.
Score 0.0: Even with help, the student cannot perform expectations.

Source: © 2019 by Fulton County Schools. Used with permission.

Figure A.1: Proficiency scale for kindergarten ELA.

GRADE 3 ELA	
Prioritized Standard: Compare and contrast the themes, settings, and plots of stories written by the same author about the same or similar characters (for example, in books from a series).	
4.0	In addition to score 3.0 performance, the student demonstrates in-depth inferences and applications that go beyond what was taught. For example, the student will: • Compare and contrast the themes, settings, and plots of two texts using textual evidence
3.5	In addition to score 3.0, in-depth inferences and applications with partial success
3.0	The student will: • Describe the similarities and differences between themes, settings, and plots of two texts The student exhibits no major errors or omissions.
2.5	No major errors or omissions regarding 2.0 content and partial knowledge of the 3.0 content
2.0	There are no major errors or omissions regarding the simpler details and processes. The student will recognize or recall specific vocabulary, such as: • *compare, contrast, plot, theme* The student will perform basic processes, such as: • Use graphic organizers to compare and contrast text plots • Identify simple themes and plots • Identify setting However, the student exhibits major errors or omissions regarding the more complex ideas and processes.
1.5	Partial knowledge of the 2.0 content but major errors or omissions regarding the 3.0 content
1.0	With help, a partial understanding of some 2.0 content (the simpler details and processes) and some 3.0 content (the more complex ideas and processes)
0.5	With help, a partial understanding of the 2.0 content but not the 3.0 content
0.0	Even with help, no understanding or skill demonstrated

Source: © 2016 by South Sioux City Community Schools. Used with permission.

Figure A.2: Proficiency scale for ELA, grade 3.

RL.5.2: DETERMINE a theme of a story, drama, or poem from details in the text, including how characters in a story or drama respond to challenges or how the speaker in a poem reflects upon a topic; **SUMMARIZE** the text.

We are learning to determine a theme (in stories, dramas, or poems).
- We are looking for details in the story or drama that support the theme (including how characters respond to challenges).
- We are looking for details in the poem that support the theme (including how the speaker reflects upon a topic).

We are learning to summarize the text.
- We are looking for a summary of the text, including key details that support the theme.

Strand: Key Ideas and Details

Topic: Analyze Theme

Grade: Fifth

4.0	In addition to 3.0, in-depth inferences and applications that go beyond what was taught	**Sample Activities** • Determine the theme of one text and identify similar themes in related texts.
3.5	In addition to 3.0 performance, in-depth inferences and applications with partial success	
3.0	**The student can:** • Support the theme with details from the story, drama, or poem • Describe how the characters respond to challenges or how the speaker reflects on a topic • Compose a summary stating the key details that support the theme	• **RL 5.7 (Analyze Nontextual Elements)—** Analyze how visual and multimedia elements contribute to the meaning, tone, or beauty of a text (for example, graphic novel, multimedia presentation of fiction, folktale, myth, or poem).
2.5	No major errors or omissions regarding 2.0 content and partial knowledge of the 3.0 content	
2.0	**The student can:** • Analyze details in the text to determine theme • Recount details of the text **Students recognize and recall vocabulary, such as:** • *summarize, topic, character traits, reflect, drama, poem, speaker, narrator, genre*	• Teach the difference between central idea, message, and theme. • **RL 5.5 (Text Structure and Relationships)—**Explain how a series of chapters, scenes, or stanzas fits together to provide the overall structure of a particular story, drama, or poem. —plot vocabulary (*exposition, inciting event, rising action, climax, falling action, resolution*)
1.5	Partial knowledge of the 2.0 content, but major errors or omissions regarding the 3.0 content	
1.0	With help, little to no understanding	

Source: © 2019 by Sheridan County School District 2. Used with permission.

Figure A.3: Proficiency scale for analyzing theme, grade 5.

WRITING: STANDARD 1 **Grade 8**		
ARGUMENT		

| **Score 4.0** | In addition to score 3.0, the student creates in-depth inferences and applies the learning.
Possibly the student will:
• Write arguments to support claims in an analysis of substantive topics or texts, using valid reasoning and relevant and sufficient evidence
    a. Introduce precise claims, distinguish the claims from alternate or opposing claims, and create an organization that establishes clear relationships among claims, counterclaims, reasons, and evidence.
    b. Develop claims and counterclaims fairly, supplying evidence for each while pointing out the strengths and limitations in a manner that anticipates the audience's knowledge level and concerns.
    c. Use words, phrases, and clauses to link the major sections of the text, create cohesions, and clarify the relationships between claims and counterclaims.
    d. Establish and maintain a formal style and objective tone while attending to the norms and conventions of the discipline in which they are writing.
    e. Provide a concluding statement or section that follows from and supports the argument presented. | |

	Score 3.5	In addition to score 3.0 performance, in-depth inferences and applications with partial success

| **Score 3.0** | The student will:
• Write arguments to support claims with clear reasons and relevant evidence
    a. Introduce claims, acknowledge and distinguish the claims from alternate or opposing claims, and organize the reasons and evidence logically.
    b. Support claims with logical reasoning and relevant evidence, using accurate, credible sources and demonstrating an understanding of the topic or text.
    c. Use words, phrases, and clauses to create cohesion and clarify the relationships between claims, counterclaims, reasons, and evidence.
    d. Establish and maintain a formal style.
    e. Provide a concluding statement or section that follows from and supports the argument presented.
*The student exhibits no major errors or omissions. | |

	Score 2.5	No major errors or omissions regarding score 2.0 content, and partial success at score 3.0 content

| **Score 2.0** | The student will:
• Write arguments to support claims with clear reasons and relevant evidence
    a. Introduce claims, acknowledge alternate or opposing claims, and organize reasons and evidence logically.
    b. Support claims with logical reasoning and relevant evidence, using accurate, credible sources and demonstrating an understanding of the topic or text.
    c. Use words, phrases, and clauses to create cohesion and clarify the relationships among claims, reasons, and evidence.
    d. Establish and maintain a formal style.
    e. Provide a concluding statement or section that follows from and supports the argument presented.
*There are no major errors or omissions regarding the simpler details and processes. However, the student exhibits major errors or omissions regarding the more complex ideas and processes. | |

	Score 1.5	Partial success at score 2.0 content, and major errors or omissions regarding score 3.0 content

Score 1.0	The student has partial understanding of some of the simpler details and processes and some of the more complex ideas and processes.
	
	Possibly the student will:
	
	• Write arguments to support claims with clear reasons and relevant evidence
	    a. Introduce claims and organize the reasons and evidence clearly.
	    b. Support claims and organize the reasons and evidence clearly.
	    c. Use words, phrases, and clauses to clarify the relationships among claim(s) and reasons.
	    d. Establish and maintain a formal style.
	    e. Provide a concluding statement or section that follows from the argument presented.	

	Score 0.5	A partial understanding of the 1.0 content
Score 0.0	No understanding or skill demonstrated	

Source: © 2016 by Laramie County School District 1. Used with permission.

Figure A.4: Proficiency scale for writing arguments, grade 8.

ENGLISH 4 **Prioritized Standard 2:** By the end of the course, the students will be able to write a personal narrative using effective techniques, well-chosen sensory details, and well-structured sequences to produce a single effect.		
Score 4.0	In addition to score 3.0 performance, the student demonstrates in-depth inferences and applications that go beyond what was taught.	
	Score 3.5	In addition to score 3.0 performance, partial success at score 4.0 content
Score 3.0	The student will: • Write a personal narrative using effective techniques, well-chosen sensory details, and well-structured sequences to produce a single effect	
	Score 2.5	No major errors or omissions regarding score 2.0 content, and partial success at score 3.0 content
Score 2.0	The student will recognize or recall specific vocabulary, such as: • *anecdote, reflection, narrative technique, sensory detail, single effect* The student will perform basic processes, such as: • Articulate the structure of a narrative piece of writing • Focus on pertinent details of an experience • Identify the relationship between an experience and its significance	
	Score 1.5	Partial success at score 2.0 content, and major errors or omissions regarding score 3.0 content
Score 1.0	With help, partial success at score 2.0 content and score 3.0 content	
	Score 0.5	With help, partial success at score 2.0 content but not at score 3.0 content
Score 0.0	Even with help, no success	

Source: © 2019 by Rutland High School. Used with permission.

Figure A.5: Proficiency scale for ELA, high school.

Subject Area and Standard or Indicator Number: GOLD 21b			
Topic: Shapes			
Score 4.0	In addition to score 3.0 performance, the student demonstrates in-depth inferences and applications that go beyond what was taught.		**Sample Activities:** • Objective 21b above level 6
	Score 3.5	In addition to score 3.0 performance, partial success at score 4.0 content	

Score 3.0	The student will:
	• Describe basic two- and three-dimensional shapes by using own words (G21b.6)
	• Recognize basic shapes when they are presented in a new orientation (G21b.6)
	  • Describe real-world objects using names of shapes.
	  • New orientation (way) or size
			Sample Activities:
			• Feely box: It has three sides and three points. It's a triangle.
			• Identifies object, then states what shape it is. "It's a ball. It rolls. It is a circle."

	Score 2.5	No major errors or omissions regarding score 2.0 content, and partial success at score 3.0 content	
Score 2.0	Student will recognize or recall specific vocabulary, such as: *heart, diamond, star, oval, square, triangle, circle, rectangle, shape, sides* There are no major errors or omissions regarding the simpler details and processes as the student: • Matches two identical shapes (G21b.2) • Identifies three basic shapes (such as heart, diamond, star, oval, square, triangle, circle, rectangle) (G21b.4) However, the student exhibits major errors or omissions regarding the more complex ideas and processes.		**Sample Activities:** • Identifies shapes in environment (for example, identifies a wheel as a circle) • Matches two identical shapes (for example, places shapes in shape-sorting box)
	Score 1.5	Partial success at score 2.0 content, and major errors or omissions regarding score 3.0 content	
Score 1.0	With help, partial success at score 2.0 content and score 3.0 content		
	Score 0.5	With help, partial success at score 2.0 content but not at score 3.0 content	

Source: © 2016 by South Sioux City Community Schools. Used with permission.

Figure A.6: Mathematics scale related to shapes, preK.

KINDERGARTEN MATH	
I can name flat and solid shapes.	
4	I can create and describe flat and solid shapes.
3	I can name flat and solid shapes.
2	I can tell the meaning of these important words: *count, flat, two-dimensional, solid, three-dimensional, shapes* I can identify shapes, such as: circle, square, triangle, rectangle, oval, rhombus, hexagon, cylinder, cone, cube, sphere.
1	I can match shapes using a visual model.

Source: © 2015 by Dawn Perez. Used with permission.

Figure A.7: Student-friendly scale for kindergarten mathematics topic of shapes.

Unit 2
Grade 4 Multi-Digit Multiplication
Score 4.0—more complex
Demonstrations of learning that go above and beyond what was explicitly taught
For example: • I can write and solve a word problem that requires multiplying a two-digit number by a two-digit number.
Score 3.0—the learning goal(s) or expectation(s) for all
• I can multiply a two-digit number by a two-digit number. • I can multiply a four-digit number by a one-digit number.
Score 2.0—the simpler stuff
Foundational knowledge, simpler procedures, isolated details, vocabulary
Essential Vocabulary: *multiply, digit, factor, product, distributive property* • I know my multiplication facts. • I can use different methods to successfully multiply. • I can multiply a two-digit number by a one-digit number. • I can use estimation to check if my answer makes sense. • I can multiply a three-digit number by a one-digit number.
Score 1.0
With help, the student can perform score 2.0 and 3.0 expectations.

Source: © 2019 by Columbus Public Schools. Used with permission.

Figure A.8: Proficiency scale for multi-digit multiplication, grade 4.

GRADE 7 ANGLES OF TRIANGLES	
Score 4.0	The student will: • Compare the angle sum of triangles to those of other polygons
Score 3.0	The student will: • Use evidence to informally explain relationships among the angles of triangles, including the sum of interior angles and angle-angle similarity
Score 2.0	The student will: • Recognize or recall specific terminology, such as: *interior angle, exterior angle, angle sum, corresponding angles, congruent,* and *similarity* The student will perform basic processes, such as: • Explain that the measures of the interior angles of a triangle add up to 180° • Explain that when two corresponding angles of two triangles are congruent, the triangles are similar
Score 1.0	With help, the student will demonstrate partial success at score 2.0 content and score 3.0 content.

Source: Adapted from Marzano, Heflebower, Hoegh, Warrick, & Grift, 2016, p. 44.

Figure A.9: Proficiency scale for angles of triangles, grade 7.

	Common Core State Standards for Mathematics Domain: Geometric Measurement and Dimension Volume (explain volume formulas and use them to solve problems) (G-GMD) High School		
Score 4.0	In addition to score 3.0, in-depth inferences and applications that go beyond instruction to the standard. The student will: • Develop an informal argument using Cavalieri's principle for the formulas for the volume of a sphere and other solid figures		**Example Activities**
	3.5	In addition to score 3.0 performance, in-depth inferences and applications with partial success	
Score 3.0	The student will: • Develop informal arguments for the formulas for the circumference of a circle, area of a circle, and volume of a cylinder, pyramid, and cone The student exhibits no major errors or omissions.		Informal Arguments–Students will be required to write an informal explanation defining the variables of the formulas for the circumference of a circle, area of a circle, and volume of a cylinder, pyramid, and cone. Having informally defined all variables of the formulas, students will be required to write an informal explanation as to why each of the formulas is true. Initially students will work individually, and then will share their thoughts with a partner. The teacher will circulate the room providing specific feedback.
	2.5	No major errors or omissions regarding 2.0 content and partial knowledge of the 3.0 content	
Score 2.0	There are no major errors or omissions regarding the simpler details and processes as the student will perform basic processes, such as: • Use the volume formulas for cylinders, pyramids, cones, and spheres to solve problems However, the student exhibits major errors or omissions regarding the more complex ideas and processes.		Volume of Pyramids, Cylinders, Cones, and Spheres—Students will be given pyramids, cylinders, cones, and spheres and be required to find the volume of each. The students will be required to work individually using the correct formula to determine the volume of each shape. The teacher will circulate the room as the students work, providing immediate and specific feedback to students. A student will get an accuracy check before moving to the next shape.
	1.5	Partial knowledge of the 2.0 content but major errors or omissions regarding the 3.0 content	
Score 1.0	With help, a partial understanding of some of the simpler details and processes and some of the more complex ideas and processes		
	0.5	With help, a partial understanding of the 2.0 content but not the 3.0 content	
Score 0.0	Even with help, no understanding or skill demonstrated		

Source: Adapted from Marzano et al., 2013, p. 248.

Figure A.10: Proficiency scale for geometric volume, high school.

EARTH AND SPACE SCIENCES

The Solar System

Grade 1

Score 4.0	In addition to score 3.0 performance, the student demonstrates in-depth inferences and applications that go beyond what was taught.	
	Score 3.5	In addition to score 3.0 performance, partial success at score 4.0 content
Score 3.0	The student will: • Make observations at different times of year to relate the amount of daylight to the time of year (for example, use observations—firsthand or from media—to make relative comparisons of the amount of daylight in the winter to the amount in the spring or fall)	
	Score 2.5	No major errors or omissions regarding score 2.0 content, and partial success at score 3.0 content
Score 2.0	The student will: • Recognize or recall specific vocabulary (for example, *comparison, daylight, fall, observation, spring, summer, sun's position, sun's size, sunrise, sunset, winter, year*) • Make and record observations of the amount of sunlight at different times of the year	
	Score 1.5	Partial success at score 2.0 content, and major errors or omissions regarding score 3.0 content
Score 1.0	With help, partial success at score 2.0 content and score 3.0 content	
	Score 0.5	With help, partial success at score 2.0 content but not at score 3.0 content
Score 0.0	Even with help, no success	

Source: Adapted from Marzano & Yanoski, 2016, p. 102.

Figure A.11: Proficiency scale for the solar system, grade 1.

Grade 3 Life Science

Prioritized Standard: Obtain, evaluate, and communicate information about the similarities and differences between the habitats found within geographical regions. Identify external features and adaptations (camouflage, use of hibernation, protection, migration, mimicry) of animals to construct an explanation of how these features and adaptations allow them to survive in their habitat.

Score 4.0: Complex Content

Demonstrations of learning that go above and beyond what was explicitly taught

For example, the student will:

- Investigate factors that contribute to the threatened or endangered status of plants or animals
- Make a claim supported by evidence to explain why one species has a more successful population than another, similar species

Score 3.0: Target Content

The expectations for all learners

The student will:

- Identify external features and adaptations (camouflage, use of hibernation, protection, migration, mimicry) of animals
- Construct an explanation of how these features and adaptations allow them to survive in their habitat

Score 2.0: Simple Content

Foundational knowledge, simpler procedures, isolated details, vocabulary

The student will recognize or recall specific vocabulary, such as:

- *adaptation, camouflage, hibernation, migration, mimicry, thrive, ecosystem, environment*

The student will perform basic processes, such as:

- Identify plants and animals that live in different habitats
- Identify how different animals and plants survive in different climates

Score 1.0

With help, the student can perform score 2.0 and 3.0 expectations.

Score 0.0

Even with help, the student cannot perform expectations.

Source: Adapted from Simms, 2016.

Figure A.12: Proficiency scale for animal adaptations to habitat, grade 3.

GRADE 4 SCIENCE

Weathering and Erosion

SCORE LEVEL	LEARNING PROGRESSION	SAMPLE ACTIVITIES
Score 4.0	The student will (for example): • Research a solution that addresses a cause of weathering and erosion	• The student will: investigate the rate of erosion by a local stream, determine how human activity impacts this rate, and implement a solution that reduces the effect of human activity, such as planting vegetation by the stream bank or maintaining a designated trail through the area.
Score 3.0	The student will: • Identify factors that contribute to weathering and erosion	• The student will: explain how weathering and erosion are caused by water, ice, wind, and vegetation, and identify factors that increase the effect and rate of weathering and erosion.
Score 2.0	The student will: • Recognize or recall specific terminology, such as: *deposition, erosion, sediment, weathering* • Explain the difference between weathering and erosion • Identify causes of weathering • Identify causes of erosion • Compare the effects of weathering and erosion over time • Explain how erosion causes deposition of weathered sediments	• The student will: recognize that weathering breaks down rocks and minerals into smaller pieces, while erosion moves the smaller pieces from place to place. • The student will: list causes of weathering, such as precipitation, ice, wind, acid rain, water, and vegetation. • The student will: list causes of erosion, such as wind, water, gravity, snow, and ice. • The student will: explain that a river may not seem to be causing erosion when observed daily, but it can carve out canyons over long spans of time.
Score 1.0	With help, the student can demonstrate partial knowledge of the score 2.0 and 3.0 content.	

Source: Adapted from Simms, 2016.

Figure A.13: Proficiency scale for weathering and erosion, grade 4.

Content Area: Science

Grade Level: Middle school

Title of Scale: Layers of the Earth

Prioritized Standard: Obtain, evaluate, and communicate information to show how Earth's surface is formed. Ask questions to compare and contrast the Earth's crust, mantle, and inner and outer core, including temperature, density, thickness, and composition.

Score 4.0: Complex Content

Demonstrations of learning that go above and beyond what was explicitly taught

For example, the student will:

- Research previous attempts made to drill to the mantle and explain the scientific reason used in the proposal (such as why one would drill through oceanic crust as opposed to continental crust)
- Develop and use a scale model of the layers of the Earth to construct an explanation of how changes in density, temperature, and composition influence the composition of the layers

Score 3.0: Target Content

The expectations for all learners

The student will:

- Ask questions to compare and contrast the different layers of the Earth in terms of temperature, density, thickness, and composition

Score 2.0: Simple Content

Foundational knowledge, simpler procedures, isolated details, vocabulary

The student will recognize or recall specific vocabulary, such as:

- *asthenosphere, composition, crust, density, inner core, lithosphere, mantle, outer core*

The student will perform basic processes, such as:

- Label the physical and chemical layers of the Earth on a diagram
- Recognize that denser substances will sink below less dense substances
- Differentiate between chemical or physical layers and compositional layers

Score 1.0

With help, the student can perform score 2.0 and 3.0 expectations.

Score 0.0

Even with help, the student cannot perform expectations.

Source: Adapted from Simms, 2016.

Figure A.14: Proficiency scale for layers of the Earth, middle school.

PHYSICAL SCIENCES		
Energy and Forces		
High School		
Score 4.0	In addition to score 3.0 performance, the student demonstrates in-depth inferences and applications that go beyond what was taught.	
	Score 3.5	In addition to score 3.0 performance, partial success at score 4.0 content
Score 3.0	The student will: **HS-PS3-5—**Develop and use a model of two objects interacting through electric or magnetic fields to illustrate the forces between objects and the changes in energy of the objects due to the interaction (for example, create a diagram, text, or drawing of two objects interacting through electric or magnetic fields—such as a drawing of what happens when two charges of opposite polarity are near each other—to show how the forces between objects and the energy of objects change as a result of the interaction)	
	Score 2.5	No major errors or omissions regarding score 2.0 content, and partial success at score 3.0 content
Score 2.0	**HS-PS3-5—**The student will: • Recognize or recall specific vocabulary (for example, *charge, electric field, energy, force, interact, magnetic field, polarity*) • Describe what happens when two objects interact through electric or magnetic fields	
	Score 1.5	Partial success at score 2.0 content, and major errors or omissions regarding score 3.0 content
Score 1.0	With help, partial success at score 2.0 content and score 3.0 content	
	Score 0.5	With help, partial success at score 2.0 content but not at score 3.0 content
Score 0.0	Even with help, no success	

Source: Adapted from Marzano & Yanoski, 2016, p. 65.

Figure A.15: Proficiency scale for energy and forces, high school.

KINDERGARTEN SOCIAL STUDIES
Topic: Community Helpers
Score 4.0
I can: • Explain the relationship between two community helpers and how their jobs are dependent on each other (for example, policemen and firemen, farmers and market)
Score 3.0
I can: • Name a community helper and describe what he or she does • Explain why a specific job in a community is important
Score 2.0
I can: • Identify multiple community helpers
Score 1.0
With help, I can do score 2.0 and score 3.0 content.

Figure A.16: Student-friendly scale for community helpers, kindergarten.

I recognize the following vocabulary terms: *colony, colonist, community, culture, immigrant, invention, Native American, natural resource, pioneer*.		I can identify habitats, resources, art, and aspects of daily lives of Native American groups.
I can explain the impact of past Americans' contributions.	**SECOND-GRADE SOCIAL STUDIES** I can compare and contrast various cultures across multiple time periods.	I can identify the contributions of one or more past Americans.
I can compare and contrast the habitats, resources, art, and daily lives of Native Americans, past and present.		I can compare and contrast the culture of people in our community across multiple time periods.

Figure A.17: Proficiency scale for comparing cultures, grade 2.

Strand: U.S. History

Topic: The Civil War

Grade 5

Score 4.0	In addition to score 3.0, the student will demonstrate in-depth inferences and applications that go beyond what was taught.	**Sample Activities**
		• Write an editorial explaining one strategy for stopping the Civil War.
Score 3.0	The student will: • Describe the growing conflict between the North and the South over the issue of slavery • Explain the political, economic, and social consequences of the Civil War	• Write a historical fiction story describing the growing conflict between the North and the South. • Create a chart organizing the consequences of the Civil War into categories (political, economic, social).

Score 2.0	The student will:
	• Recognize or recall specific terminology, such as:
	  • *conflict, consequence, Reconstruction*
	• Perform basic processes, such as:
	  • Identify causes of the Civil War
	  • Identify consequences of the Civil War
		• Select causes of the growing conflict between the North and the South from a teacher-provided list.
		• Using a true/false format, determine if a statement is a consequence of the Civil War.

Score 1.0	With help, the student demonstrates partial understanding of score 2.0 and score 3.0.	

Figure A.18: Proficiency scale for the Civil War, grade 5.

Course: American Government **Topic:** State Government **High School**
Prioritized Standard: The student will demonstrate knowledge of the federal system of government described in the United States Constitution and explain the relationship of state governments to the national government.
Score 4.0
The student will: • Explain how the federal government has used fiscal federalism to increase its influence over state decision making. Cite specific evidence to support this claim.
Score 3.0
The student will: • Explain the relationship of state governments to the national government • Identify the reserved, exclusive, and concurrent powers of state and national governments • Describe the difference between dual and cooperative federalism
Score 2.0
The student will: • Explain how local governments are formed from state governments • Explain states' responsibilities regarding education, marriage licenses, and criminal law • Identify the differences between dual and cooperative federalism

Source: © 2019 by Fulton County Schools. Used with permission.

Figure A.19: Proficiency scale for state government, high school.

Strand: History
Topic: Chronological Thinking
Grade: High School

12.4.1 Students will analyze how major past and current events are chronologically connected and evaluate their impact on one another.

Score 4.0	In addition to score 3.0, in-depth inferences and applications that go beyond what was taught • Identify two events from the same time period that had significant impact. Identify which event had more impact and provide evidence to support the decision.	**Sample Activities**
	3.5 In addition to score 3.0 performance, in-depth inferences and applications with partial success	
Score 3.0	The student will: • Relate past and present events to one another • Critique the effects of past and present events • Predict plausible future outcomes based on past events The student exhibits no major errors or omissions.	• WWII Timeline Activity–relate events within time frame and extend to predict future outcomes. • Edison Timeline–predict and explain the effects of major inventions.
	2.5 No major errors or omissions regarding 2.0 content and partial knowledge of the 3.0 content	

Score 2.0	There are no major errors or omissions regarding the simpler details and processes as the student:
	• Recognizes or recalls specific terminology, such as:
	  ‣ *chronological*
	• Performs basic processes, such as:
	  ‣ Describe relevant past and present events
	However, the student exhibits major errors or omissions regarding the more complex ideas and processes.
		• WWII Timeline Activity–describe events from WWII.
		• Edison Timeline–identify major inventions.

	1.5 Partial knowledge of the 2.0 content, but major errors or omissions regarding the 3.0 content	
Score 1.0	With help, a partial understanding of some of the simpler details and processes and some of the more complex ideas and processes	
	0.5 With help, a partial understanding of the 2.0 content, but not the 3.0 content	
Score 0.0	Even with help, no understanding or skill demonstrated	

Source: © 2016 by South Sioux City Community Schools. Used with permission.

Figure A.20: Proficiency scale for chronological thinking, high school.

	Grade 1 Music Theory
4	• I can create and perform a four-beat rhythm pattern using the pitches so-mi.
3	• I can perform a steady beat or rhythm using *ta*, *ti-ti*, and *sh*. • I can perform piano and forte. • I can sing the pitches so-mi using a pleasing voice.
2	• I can define important music terms, including: *rhythm, piano, forte, pitch.*
1	• With help, I can demonstrate partial success of scores 2 and 3.

Source: © 2019 by Columbus Public Schools. Used with permission.

Figure A.21: Proficiency scale for music theory, grade 1.

	Improvements in Technology Grades K-2
4	I can critique one specific example of how technology has changed life and justify whether it has resulted in more positive or negative effects, citing specific examples for each.
3	I can identify examples of how technology has changed. The student will explain how technology changes have improved how people live, work, and communicate.
2	I can list ways technology is commonly used at home and in school.
1	With help, I can demonstrate partial success of scores 2 and 3.

Source: Simms, 2016.

Figure A.22: Proficiency scale for improvements in technology, grades K–2.

	Learning Goal: I will practice safe behaviors when online.
4	I will: • Consistently model safe online behaviors • Be an upstander for myself and others
3	I will: • Explain what to do about cyberbullying • Identify what is safe and unsafe to share online • Explain what to do if a pop-up appears
2	I will: • Define *cyberbullying, netiquette, appropriate, upstander* • List personal information I should not share online • Ask for help when I feel sad, scared, or uncomfortable online • Ask permission to be online • Only talk to people online that I know • Only go to places online that are right for me
1	I will: • Be safe online only with adult guidance

Source: © 2019 by Columbus Public Schools. Used with permission.

Figure A.23: Proficiency scale for online safety, grades K–2.

Grade 4: Counseling

Topic: Bullying

The student will demonstrate advocacy skills and ability to assert self, when necessary.

Student-friendly learning goals:
- I can demonstrate helpful strategies in any role within a bullying situation.
- I can give examples of how roles in bullying may change with each bullying situation.
- I can name strategies that are helpful in a bullying situation.

1	2	3	4
I do not know helpful strategies for a bullying situation.	I know helpful strategies for a bullying situation, but I do not use them.	I use helpful strategies in any role of a bullying situation; target, bystander, bully.	I encourage others to use helpful strategies in bullying situations.

Source: © 2019 by Columbus Public Schools. Used with permission.

Figure A.24: Proficiency scale for preventing bullying, grade 4.

MIDDLE SCHOOL BAND		
Level 4.0	In addition to level 3.0 performance, the student will: • Critique his or her own performance in order to improve its quality	
	Level 3.5	In addition to level 3.0 performance, the student shows partial success at level 4.
Level 3.0	The student will: • Perform on instruments through a varied repertoire of music, alone and with others • Demonstrate ensemble skills through performance of musical literature (for example, dynamic expressions, style, blend and balance, steady tempo, rhythmic accuracy, intonation)	
	Level 2.5	The student is successful with level 2.0 elements and partially successful with level 3.0 elements.
Level 2.0	The student will recognize or recall specific vocabulary, such as: *long tones, lip slurs, chorales, major scales, chromatic scale, technique, conductor cues, dynamic expression, style, blend and balance, steady tempo, rhythmic accuracy, intonation.* The student will perform basic processes, such as: • Demonstrate proper warm-up techniques (for example, long tones, lip slurs, chorales, major scales, chromatic, scale, technical exercises)	
	Level 1.5	The student is partially successful with level 2.0 elements without prompting.
Level 1.0	With prompting, the student is partially successful with level 2.0 elements.	

Source: © 2019 by Fulton County Schools. Used with permission.

Figure A.25: Proficiency scale for middle school band.

Topic: Art

Grade Level or Course: Seventh Grade

Standard: Students will create, perform, exhibit, or participate in the arts.

Score 4.0: Complex Content

Demonstrations of learning that go above and beyond what was explicitly taught

The student will (for example):

- Analyze the use of the elements and principles of design in their artwork and the artwork of others

---

Score 3.0: Target Content

The expectations for all students

The student will:

- Compose with the elements of art and principles of design to communicate ideas into an original work of art
- Prepare and exhibit his or her artwork

Score 2.0: Simple Content

Foundational knowledge, simpler procedures, isolated details, vocabulary

The student will recognize or recall specific vocabulary, such as:

- *brainstorming list, cliché symbol, media/medium, mind-mapping, plagiarism, thumbnail sketch*

The student will perform basic processes, such as:

- Compose a series of ideas to create original works of art (for example, three different sketches for one idea, evolving sketches for one idea, or multiple separate sketches for multiple separate ideas)
- Demonstrate knowledge of various elements of art and principles of design

---

Score 1.0: With help, the student can perform score 2.0 and 3.0 expectations.

Score 0.0: Even with help, the student cannot perform expectations.

Figure A.26: Proficiency scale for art, grade 7.

High School World Language—Level 2			
Culture			
Score 4.0	In addition to score 3.0, in-depth inferences and applications that go beyond instruction to the standard. The student will: • Create a cultural representation of the topic applied in our own culture • Critique why certain cultural concepts learned would not work in another culture, providing evidence to support your position • Discuss ways cultural differences inform behaviors and language • Design a cultural activity different from one studied in class		**Sample Activities**
	3.5	In addition to score 3.0 performance, in-depth inferences and applications with partial success	
Score 3.0	The student will: • Compare and contrast different cultures, including practices, products, and perspectives • Develop a logical argument on why the practices, products, and perspectives discussed may or may not work in another culture • Cite evidence as to how practices, products, and perspectives are used in another culture		• Compare and contrast target culture with native or other cultural community. • Create a pamphlet or booklet on helpful hints for a traveler in that country. • Using evidence in class discussion, hypothesize why certain behaviors would be or not be acceptable or appropriate in one culture but not in another.
	2.5	No major errors or omissions regarding 2.0 content and partial knowledge of the 3.0 content	
Score 2.0	There are no major errors or omissions regarding the simpler details and processes as the student will perform basic processes, such as: • Identify differences across cultures • Identify ways that cultural differences are manifested		• List differences between native and target cultures. • Recall cultural topic information discussed in class.
	1.5	Partial knowledge of the 2.0 content but major errors or omissions regarding the 3.0 content	
Score 1.0	With help, a partial understanding of some of the simpler details and processes and some of the more complex ideas and processes		

Figure A.27: Proficiency scale for world languages and culture, high school.

Topic: Entrepreneurship

Grade Level or Course: High School

Standard: Students will understand the concepts, systems, and strategies needed to acquire, motivate, develop, and terminate employees.

Score 4.0: Complex Content

Demonstrations of learning that go above and beyond what was explicitly taught

The student will (for example):

- Create an on-boarding process for new employees
- Evaluate the support provided for an employee
- Research and describe critical cultural attributes of any work environment

---

Score 3.0: Target Content

The expectations for all students

The student will:

- Describe quality hiring practices
- Explain how to coach employees to ensure success in the work environment

---

Score 2.0: Simple Content

Foundational knowledge, simpler procedures, isolated details, vocabulary

The student will recognize or recall specific vocabulary, such as:

- *on-boarding, organizational culture*

The student will perform basic processes, such as:

- Compare and contrast the various types of work arrangements (for example, flextime, compressed work week, job sharing)
- Identify reasons for firing an employee
- Identify reasons for hiring an employee

Score 1.0: With help, the student can perform score 2.0 and 3.0 expectations.

Score 0.0: Even with help, the student cannot perform expectations.

Source: © 2019 by Fulton County Schools. Used with permission.

Figure A.28: Proficiency scale for entrepreneurship, high school.

Employability Skills Rubric (Secondary)
Students demonstrate employability skills.

Student Name:
Date:
Performance Assessment: Beginning   Middle   End

	Score 4.0 Exceeding	Score 3.0 Meeting	Score 2.0 Developing	Score 1.0 Beginning
SOCIAL CONDUCT	• Arrives on time prepared for class every day • Participates every day; actions drive instruction forward • Consistently does what is expected and helps others do the same	• Arrives on time prepared for class consistently • Participates in class; actions benefit instruction • Accepts responsibility for actions and rarely requires redirection	• Arrives on time prepared for class inconsistently • Participates in class; actions at times distract instruction • Usually follows redirection and changes actions	• Rarely brings materials to class, even with teacher coaching • Rarely participates; comments often distract from instruction • Does not follow redirection to change actions

Your Rating and Reason:

Teaching Rating:

WORK COMPLETION	• Completes work as assigned every day • Routinely submits work on time • Takes full advantage of reassessment opportunities and support • Goes beyond expectations or demonstrates initiative	• Consistently completes work as assigned • Usually submits work on time • Takes advantage of reassessment opportunities and support	• Inconsistently completes work as assigned • Inconsistently submits work on time • Occasionally takes advantage of reassessment opportunities and support	• Rarely completes work as assigned • Rarely submits work on time • Rarely takes advantage of reassessment opportunities and support

Your Rating and Reason:

Teaching Rating:

continued ⇨

WORKING WITH ADULTS	• Assumes responsibility for learning by seeking help and asking questions in a timely manner • Consistently listens and follows suggestions given by adults • Consistently demonstrates effective communication skills and willingness to work with adults	• Usually assumes responsibility for learning by seeking help and asking questions when needed • Usually listens and follows suggestions given by adults • Usually demonstrates effective communication skills and willingness to work with adults	• Occasionally seeks help and asks questions when needed • Inconsistently listens and follows suggestions given by adults • Sometimes demonstrates effective communication skills and willingness to work with adults	• Rarely seeks help and asks questions when needed • Rarely listens and follows suggestions given by adults • Rarely demonstrates effective communication skills and willingness to work with adults
Your Rating and Reason: **Teaching Rating:**				
WORKING WITH STUDENTS	• Effectively leads a group of students • Can help resolve most conflicts • Seeks out different points of view • Embraces diversity in others	• Effectively communicates with other students • Does not participate in conflicts • Accepts different points of view • Accepts diversity in others	• Occasionally communicates effectively with other students • Does not escalate conflicts • Occasionally accepts different points of view • Occasionally accepts diversity in others	• Does not communicate effectively with other students • Escalates conflicts • Does not accept different points of view • Does not accept diversity in others
Your Rating and Reason: **Teaching Rating:**				

Source: © 2019 by Uinta County School District #1. Created by the Secondary Vocational Collaborative Team. Used with permission.

Figure A.29: Proficiency scale for employability, secondary.

HIGH SCHOOL		
Effective Collaboration Scale		
Level 4.0	In addition to level 3.0 performance, the student will: • Critique his or her own collaborative behaviors by identifying personal strengths and areas of growth as a collaborative team member	
	Level 3.5	In addition to level 3.0 performance, the student shows partial success at level 4.
Level 3.0	The student will use all level 2.0 collaborative skills with consistency to: • Engage collaboratively in small-group activities • Contribute in a meaningful way to whole-class discussions	
	Level 2.5	The student is successful with level 2.0 elements and partially successful with level 3.0 elements.
Level 2.0	The student is successful with the simpler details and behaviors, such as: • Define the concept of collaboration • Explain why it is necessary for group production • Explain specific active listening behaviors for small-group and class discussions • Identify conversation prompts for appropriate and productive agreement or disagreement within small-group or whole-class discussion	
	Level 1.5	The student is partially successful with level 2.0 elements without prompting.
Level 1.0	With prompting, the student is partially successful with level 2.0 elements.	
	Level 0.5	With help or prompting, the student is partially successful with level 2.0 elements.

Figure A.30: Proficiency scale for effective collaboration, high school.

APPENDIX B

Common Scale Templates With Examples

This appendix presents reproducible templates for common proficiency scale formats; each one is followed by a sample scale that illustrates how it will look when filled in with specific content. Visit **MarzanoResources .com/reproducibles** to download each scale and template.

Proficiency Scale With Sample Activities

Standard:	
Topic:	
Grade and Course:	

			Sample Activities
Score 4.0	In addition to score 3.0, in-depth inferences and applications that go beyond what was taught The student will: • •		
	3.5	In addition to score 3.0 performance, in-depth inferences and applications with partial success	
Score 3.0	The student will: • • • The student exhibits no major errors or omissions.		

A Handbook for Developing and Using Proficiency Scales in the Classroom © 2020 Marzano Resources • MarzanoResources.com
Visit **MarzanoResources.com/reproducibles** to download this free reproducible.

	2.5	No major errors or omissions regarding 2.0 content and partial knowledge of the 3.0 content	
Score 2.0		There are no major errors or omissions regarding the simpler details and processes as the student: • Recognizes or recalls specific terminology, such as: 　　• • Performs basic processes, such as: 　　• 　　• However, the student exhibits major errors or omissions regarding the more complex ideas and processes.	
	1.5	Partial knowledge of the 2.0 content, but major errors or omissions regarding the 3.0 content	
Score 1.0		With help, a partial understanding of some of the simpler details and processes and some of the more complex ideas and processes	
	0.5	With help, a partial understanding of the 2.0 content, but not the 3.0 content	
Score 0.0		Even with help, no understanding or skill demonstrated	

A Handbook for Developing and Using Proficiency Scales in the Classroom © 2020 Marzano Resources • MarzanoResources.com
Visit **MarzanoResources.com/reproducibles** to download this free reproducible.

Standard: Measurement

Topic: Word Problems With Money

Grade: Second

Score 4.0	In addition to score 3.0, in-depth inferences and applications that go beyond what was taught, such as the following. The student will: • Write, solve, and share a multi-step word problem involving dollar bills, quarters, dimes, nickels, and pennies • Count back change for values up to $10.00		**Sample Activities**
	3.5	In addition to score 3.0 performance, in-depth inferences and applications with partial success	
Score 3.0	The student will: • Solve word problems involving dollar bills, quarters, dimes, nickels, and pennies The student exhibits no major errors or omissions.		• **Shopping activity:** Materials for each pair: word problems involving buying things, coins, dollar bills, white boards, markers, erasers Procedures: Students work with a partner. One partner is the buyer, and the other partner is the seller. The buyer draws a card, reads the problem, and solves it on the white board, using the money if needed to solve the problem. The seller checks the answer to be sure it is correct. The partners switch roles and play again. They continue playing, taking turns as the buyer and the seller.
	2.5	No major errors or omissions regarding 2.0 content and partial knowledge of the 3.0 content	

Score 2.0	There are no major errors or omissions regarding the simpler details and processes as the student:
	• Recognizes or recalls specific terminology, such as:
	   • *all together, coin, decimal, remaining, value*
	• Performs basic processes, such as:
	   • Identify coin values (quarter, dime, nickel, penny)
	   • Use $ and ¢ symbols appropriately
	   • Add or subtract different coins to determine a total amount of money or money remaining
	However, the student exhibits major errors or omissions regarding the more complex ideas and processes.
			• Students match pictures of coins with cards displaying values (picture of quarter = $.25 or 25¢).

	1.5	Partial knowledge of the 2.0 content, but major errors or omissions regarding the 3.0 content
Score 1.0	With help, a partial understanding of some of the simpler details and processes and some of the more complex ideas and processes	
	0.5	With help, a partial understanding of the 2.0 content, but not the 3.0 content
Score 0.0	Even with help, no understanding or skill demonstrated	

Source: Adapted from Marzano, R. J., Yanoski, D. C., Hoegh, J. K., & Simms, J. A. (2013). Using Common Core standards to enhance classroom instruction and assessment. *Bloomington, IN: Marzano Resources, p. 264.*

Proficiency Scale With Whole-Number Scores Only

Content Area:

Grade Level:

Title of Scale:

Prioritized Standard:
Score 4.0: Complex Content Demonstrations of learning that go above and beyond what was explicitly taught For example, the student will: • •
Score 3.0: Target Content The expectations for all learners The student will: • •
Score 2.0: Simple Content Foundational knowledge, simpler procedures, isolated details, vocabulary The student will recognize or recall specific vocabulary, such as: • The student will perform basic processes, such as: • • •
Score 1.0 With help, the student can perform score 2.0 and 3.0 expectations.
Score 0.0 Even with help, the student cannot perform expectations.

Content Area: Science

Grade Level: Fourth

Title of Scale: Animal adaptations

Prioritized Standard: Obtain, evaluate, and communicate information about the similarities and differences between the habitats found within geographical regions. Identify external features and adaptations (camouflage, use of hibernation, protection, migration, mimicry) of animals to construct an explanation of how these features and adaptations allow them to survive in their habitat.

Score 4.0: Complex Content

Demonstrations of learning that go above and beyond what was explicitly taught

For example, the student will:

- Investigate factors that contribute to the threatened or endangered status of plants or animals
- Make a claim supported by evidence to explain why one species has a more successful population than another similar species

---

Score 3.0: Target Content

The expectations for all learners

The student will:

- Identify external features and adaptations (camouflage, use of hibernation, protection, migration, mimicry) of animals.
- Construct an explanation of how these features and adaptations allow them to survive in their habitat

---

Score 2.0: Simple Content

Foundational knowledge, simpler procedures, isolated details, vocabulary

The student will recognize or recall specific vocabulary, such as:

- *adaptation, camouflage, hibernation, migration, mimicry, thrive, ecosystem, environment*

The student will perform basic processes, such as:

- Identify plants and animals that live in different habitats
- Identify how different animals and plants survive in different climates

---

Score 1.0

With help, the student can perform score 2.0 and 3.0 expectations.

Score 0.0

Even with help, the student cannot perform expectations.

Source: Adapted from Simms, J. A. (2016). The critical concepts. Accessed at www.MarzanoResources.com/the-critical-concepts on February 21, 2019.

Proficiency Scale With Accommodations and Modifications

Content Area:

Grade Level:

Title of Scale:

	Proficiency Scale	Accommodations	Modifications
4.0	In addition to score 3.0 performance, the student demonstrates in-depth inferences and applications that go beyond what was taught. For example, the student will: •		
3.5	In addition to score 3.0, in-depth inferences and applications with partial success		
3.0	The student will: • • •		
2.5	No major errors or omissions regarding 2.0 content and partial knowledge of the 3.0 content		
2.0	There are no major errors or omissions regarding the simpler details and processes. The student will recognize or recall specific vocabulary, such as: • The student will perform basic processes, such as: • • •		
1.5	Partial knowledge of the 2.0 content but major errors or omissions regarding the 3.0 content		
1.0	With help, a partial understanding of some 2.0 content (the simpler details and processes) and some 3.0 content (the more complex ideas and processes)		
0.5	With help, a partial understanding of the 2.0 content but not the 3.0 content		
0.0	Even with help, no understanding or skill demonstrated		

A Handbook for Developing and Using Proficiency Scales in the Classroom © 2020 Marzano Resources • MarzanoResources.com
Visit **MarzanoResources.com/reproducibles** to download this free reproducible.

Content Area: Social Studies
Grade Level: Third Grade
Title of Scale: American Indian Cultures (Gifted and Talented)

Prioritized Standard: Describe early American Indian cultures and their development in North America.

	Proficiency Scale	Accommodations	Modifications
4.0	In addition to score 3.0 performance, the student demonstrates in-depth inferences and applications that go beyond what was taught. For example, the student will: • Gather, analyze, and organize information from multiple sources on American Indians, then compare and contrast to other groups (such as Native Americans and European colonists)	The student will be provided the following accommodations, as needed: • Provide resources and materials for the student to choose from in order for him or her to independently complete the level 4.0 task	The student will: • Communicate in a self-selected manner how contributions made by American Indians have impacted his or her life, including whether or not the impact is positive or negative and why
3.5	In addition to score 3.0, in-depth inferences and applications with partial success.		
3.0	The student will: • Explain how and why the contributions made by American Indians are still being used today The student exhibits no major errors or omissions.	The student will be provided the following accommodations, as needed: • Provide resources and materials for the student to choose from in order for him or her to independently explain how and why contributions made by American Indians are still being used today	The student will: • Gather, analyze, and organize information from multiple sources on American Indians, then compare and contrast to other groups (such as Native Americans and European colonists)
2.5	No major errors or omissions regarding 2.0 content and partial knowledge of the 3.0 content		
2.0	There are no major errors or omissions regarding the simpler details and processes. The student will perform basic processes, such as: • Identify the regions in which American Indians settled (Arctic, Northwest, Southwest, Plains, Northeast, and Southeast) • Describe how American Indian groups used their environment to obtain food, clothing, and shelter • Compare and contrast how American Indian groups used their environments to obtain food, clothing, and shelter However, the student exhibits major errors or omissions regarding the more complex ideas and processes.	The student will be provided the following accommodations, as needed: • Provide resources and materials for the student to choose from in order for him or her to independently gain knowledge related to the level 2.0 content	The student will: • Explain how and why the contributions made by American Indians are still being used today
1.5	Partial knowledge of the 2.0 content but major errors or omissions regarding the 3.0 content		
1.0	With help, a partial understanding of some 2.0 content (the simpler details and processes) and some 3.0 content (the more complex ideas and processes)		
0.5	With help, a partial understanding of the 2.0 content but not the 3.0 content		
0.0	Even with help, no understanding or skill demonstrated		

page 2 of 2

Proficiency Scale for Multiple Topics

Content Area:

Grade Level and Course:

Title of Scale:

Measurement Topics	Learning Targets	Score 4.0	Score 3.0	Score 2.0	Score 1.0

Content Area: Mathematics

Grade Level and Course: Grade 8, Algebra 2

Title of Scale: Absolute Value Function

Measurement Topics	Learning Targets	Score 4.0	Score 3.0	Score 2.0	Score 1.0
Function Attributes	The student will: • Identify the mathematical domains and ranges of functions • Determine reasonable domain and range values for continuous and discrete situations • Identify and sketch graphs of parent functions, including the absolute value of x	• Justify why a problem situation is modeled by the absolute value function.	• Identify mathematical domain and range of functions and determine reasonable domain and range values for given situations, both continuous and discrete. • Identify and sketch the graph of parent functions.	• Identify the mathematics domain and range of functions for discrete situations or continuous with some incorrect values or incorrect notation. • Identify OR graph the absolute value parent function.	• With help, the student can demonstrate partial knowledge of the score 2.0 and score 3.0 content.
Solving Absolute Value Functions	The student will: • Create and interpret scatter plots • Analyze situations and formulate systems of equations with two or more unknowns	• Create a problem situation which is modeled in scatter plots. • Predict future behavior of the function as applied to real-world applications. • Solve an absolute value function.	• Interpret a set of data, make a scatter plot, and create a function that fits the data most accurately. • Predict future values. • Write the absolute value equation as two separate linear equations.	• Sketch a scatter plot given a table of data and describe its correlation. • Write an equation to solve the absolute value function.	• With help, the student can demonstrate partial knowledge of the score 2.0 and score 3.0 content.
Transformation With Absolute Value Function	The student will: • Extend parent functions with parameters • Describe the effects of the parameter changes on the graph of parent functions		• Describe ALL effects of a, h, and k transformations on the graph of the absolute value function.	• Describe transformations using a, h, OR k, but not all on the graph of the absolute value function.	• With help, the student can demonstrate partial knowledge of the score 2.0 and score 3.0 content.

Source: © 2015 by Mario Acosta. Used with permission.

page 2 of 2

APPENDIX C
Scale Development Checklists

This appendix presents reproducible checklists for developing proficiency scales. Visit **MarzanoResources .com/reproducibles** to download this reproducible.

Scale Development Checklists

Criteria for Prioritizing Standards

Consider the following criteria when determining which standards are critical to a particular grade level or course and should therefore be the subject of proficiency scales.

Prioritized Standards Review
Criteria for Priority
Teacher Judgment
Includes knowledge and skills that are considered very important (nonnegotiable) by the content expert or teacher
Assessment Connected
Includes content that will likely be included on a classroom, district, or large-scale assessment
Endurance
Includes knowledge and skills that will last beyond a grade level or course
Leverage
Includes knowledge and skills that cross over into multiple domains
Readiness
Includes knowledge and skills that are important to success in a subsequent course

- ❑ Does the standard meet any criteria for priority? How many?
- ❑ Is mastery of the standard necessary for another standard addressed in the course or for a following course?
- ❑ Is the standard so important that it receives significant instructional time and is formally assessed?
- ❑ Is the standard so important that it requires being articulated in a learning progression on a proficiency scale?
- ❑ Is the prioritized standard tested on the high-stakes assessment?

Guidance for Writing High-Quality Proficiency Scales

Consider each guideline in this document as you write and refine proficiency scales to ensure high quality.

Score 4.0	This level is in addition to score 3.0 performance. The student demonstrates in-depth inferences and applications that go beyond what was taught. • Include an example or two of how a student might demonstrate a performance beyond the expectation of the standard. • Be sure the cognitive demand of the content at this level exceeds that of score 3.0. • Remember that a student can demonstrate a performance at this level in a variety of ways, but often these tasks require problem solving, decision making, experimentation, or investigation.
Score 3.0	This level articulates the expectation for ALL students and aligns to the priority standard. • Ensure that each bullet is a required expectation at the level of the standard. • Be sure the cognitive demand of the content at this level exceeds that of score 2.0. • Consider supporting standards content to be included at this level (if directly related to the priority standard). • Remember that each bullet requires explicit classroom instruction. • Limit the number of bullets at this level to three, if possible.
Score 2.0	This level includes simple content related to the priority standard. • Include critical vocabulary terms related to the standard. • Articulate the simple content within the standard, or the prerequisite knowledge and skills, but be sure to be selective and purposeful in making decisions about what is included on the scale. • Each bullet at score 3.0 typically has a related bullet at score 2.0 (but not required). • Consider previous and following grade-level expectations when determining the prerequisite knowledge and skills. • Consider supporting standards content to be included at this level (if directly related to the priority standard). • Limit the number of bullets at this level to three, if possible, not including the vocabulary terms.

A Handbook for Developing and Using Proficiency Scales in the Classroom © 2020 Marzano Resources • MarzanoResources.com
Visit **MarzanoResources.com/reproducibles** to download this free reproducible.

Proficiency Scale Review Checklist

Content Area: _____

Grade Level and Standard: _____

Criteria	Yes	No	Comments
Specificity The language of each level on the scale is clear and specific. Each learning target is a single-idea statement of intended knowledge gain.			
Progression Verbs are present, and these verbs and corresponding context represent a progression of complexity from score 2.0 to score 4.0.			
Comprehensiveness The proficiency scale is achievable. It has enough depth, yet not so much to warrant an additional scale. Each level on the scale includes one to three related learning targets.			
Measurability Each learning target is observable and quantifiable.			
Format Each learning target is written with the verb first to provide focus on what the student should know or be able to do.			
Vocabulary Key vocabulary has been identified at the score 2.0 level.			
Prerequisites Prerequisite knowledge and skills have been identified at the score 2.0 level.			
Rigor Score 3.0 aligns closely to the standard represented on the scale. The cognitive demand at score 3.0 aligns to the expectations of the standard.			
Alignment The scale is aligned vertically with previous and subsequent grade levels or courses.			

APPENDIX D
Score 4.0 Examples

The examples in this appendix display score 3.0 learning goals and corresponding score 4.0 content.

GRADE 7 ENGLISH LANGUAGE ARTS	
Score 4.0	The student will (for example): • Identify two competing claims about a text, support each with textual evidence, and explain which of the claims is better supported
Score 3.0	The student will: • Make claims about what a specific text says explicitly • Use relevant textual evidence to support those claims

Source: Adapted from Marzano et al., 2016, p. 45.

Figure D.1: Sample score 4.0 content for ELA, grade 7.

ALGEBRA 1	
Score 4.0	The student will (for example): • Solve compound inequalities • Solve absolute value equations and inequalities • Write and solve equations for real-world situations and consecutive integers
Score 3.0	The student will: • Solve linear equations with one variable • Solve linear inequalities with one variable

Source: © 2019 by Columbus Public Schools. Used with permission.

Figure D.2: Sample score 4.0 content for algebra 1.

GRADE 4 SCIENCE	
Score 4.0	The student will (for example): • Research and describe a solution that addresses a cause of weathering and erosion
Score 3.0	The student will: • Describe factors that contribute to weathering and erosion

Source: Adapted from Simms, 2016.

Figure D.3: Sample score 4.0 content for science, grade 4.

MIDDLE SCHOOL ART	
Score 4.0	The student will (for example): • Create a three-dimensional piece of art using advanced shapes (for example, rhombus, trapezoid, organic)
Score 3.0	The student will: • Create a three-dimensional one-point perspective piece of art using value and space

Source: © 2019 by Columbus Public Schools. Used with permission.

Figure D.4: Sample score 4.0 content for middle school art.

KINDERGARTEN SOCIAL STUDIES	
Score 4.0	The student will (for example): • Explain the effect (problem) that might occur if a good or service was not provided in the community
Score 3.0	The student will: • Explain how money is used to purchase goods and services

Source: © 2019 by Fulton County Schools. Used with permission.

Figure D.5: Sample score 4.0 content for social studies, kindergarten.

SPANISH 1	
Score 4.0	The student will (for example): • Present information about self-selected topics using a variety of phrases and simple sentences • Give simple presentations on a teacher-determined or self-selected cultural topic
Score 3.0	The student will: • Present information about self and other familiar topics using a variety of words, phrases, and memorized expressions • Participate in simple dialogue

Source: © 2016 by South Sioux City Community Schools. Used with permission.

Figure D.6: Sample score 4.0 content for Spanish 1.

GRADE 3 MUSIC	
Score 4.0	The student will (for example): • Describe how a composer's music impacts emotion (how he or she feels or what he or she thinks as a result of listening to the music)
Score 3.0	The student will: • Recall facts about selected composers • Describe melodies from selected composers

Source: © 2019 by Columbus Public Schools. Used with permission.

Figure D.7: Sample score 4.0 content for music, grade 3.

GRADE 5 PHYSICAL EDUCATION	
Score 4.0	The student will (for example): In addition to score 3.0, demonstrate a higher level of performance for movement skills and patterns
Score 3.0	The student will: • Demonstrate grade-appropriate movement skills and patterns in a variety of activities • The following skills are required to earn a score 3.0 in the unit on soccer: ▪ Dribbling—Keeps the ball moving between feet ▪ Passing—Stops, plants one foot on the ground, and kicks the ball using the inside of the free foot to target ▪ Receiving—Plants one foot on the ground, and stops the ball with the inside of the other foot ▪ Throwing—Places both hands on the outside of the ball, and overhand throws to the target

Source: © 2019 by Uinta County School District #1. Created by the Physical Education Collaborative Team. Used with permission.

Figure D.8: Sample score 4.0 content for physical education, grade 5.

Scales With Sample Assessments

The examples in this appendix present a proficiency scale and related assessment items.

Comparing Fractions

Prioritized Standard: Compare two fractions with different numerators and different denominators using <, >, and =, and justify the comparison.

Scale

NUMBER AND QUANTITY Compare Fractions Grade 4	
Score 4.0	In addition to score 3.0 performance, the student demonstrates in-depth inferences and applications that go beyond what was taught. For example, given three or more fractions with different denominators, the student orders them least to greatest or greatest to least. For example, the student compares improper and mixed fractions with unlike denominators.
Score 3.0	The student: • Compares two fractions with different numerators and different denominators using <, >, and = • Justifies the comparison
Score 2.0	The student recognizes or recalls specific vocabulary, such as: • *compare, comparison, denominator, equivalent, fraction, generate, justify, numerator* The student performs basic processes, such as: • Recognizes symbols, such as <, >, and = • Recognizes and generates equivalent fractions • Compares two fractions with like denominators
Score 1.0	With help, the student demonstrates partial success at score 2.0 and score 3.0.

Source: © 2019 by Clark-Pleasant Community School Corporation. Used with permission.

Figure E.1: Proficiency scale for comparing fractions, grade 4.

Assessment

Name:	Teacher:

Compare two fractions with different numerators and different denominators using <, >, and =, and justify the comparison.			
Score 2.0: Write <, >, or = for each pair of fractions.			
1. $\dfrac{3}{4}$ ___ $\dfrac{2}{4}$	2. $\dfrac{6}{8}$ ___ $\dfrac{7}{8}$	3. $\dfrac{1}{8}$ ___ $\dfrac{4}{8}$	4. $\dfrac{3}{6}$ ___ $\dfrac{2}{6}$
Score 3.0: Write <, >, or = for each pair of fractions. Justify your answer with work, pictures, or words.			
5. $\dfrac{3}{4}$ ___ $\dfrac{4}{5}$	6. $\dfrac{1}{3}$ ___ $\dfrac{2}{7}$	7. $\dfrac{5}{6}$ ___ $\dfrac{7}{8}$	8. $\dfrac{2}{3}$ ___ $\dfrac{4}{6}$
Score 4.0: Solve the story problem below. Justify your answer with work, pictures, or words.			
9. Cindy feeds her cats Fluffy, Mittens, and Spots each day. Fluffy eats $2\frac{1}{2}$ cups of food each day. Mittens eats $2\frac{5}{6}$ cups of food each day. Spots eats $2\frac{1}{4}$ cups of food each day. Put the cats' names in order from least to greatest according to how much they eat each day.			

Source: © 2019 by Clark-Pleasant Community School Corporation. Used with permission.

Figure E.2: Sample assessment for comparing fractions, grade 4.

Claims, Evidence, and Reasoning

Prioritized Standard: The student will make claims about what a specific text says explicitly and use relevant textual evidence to support those claims.

Scale

Score 4.0—more complex
Demonstrations of learning that go beyond what was explicitly taught
The student will:
• Identify two competing claims about a text, support each with textual evidence, and explain which of the claims is better supported

Score 3.0—the learning goals or expectations for all students
The student will:
• Make claims about what a specific text says explicitly
• Use relevant textual evidence to support those claims

Score 2.0—the simpler stuff

Foundational knowledge, simpler procedures, isolated details, vocabulary

The student will:

- Recognize or recall specific vocabulary, such as: *claim, explicitly, inference, relevant, textual evidence*
- Identify or recognize claims that are supported by textual evidence provided by the teacher
- Locate or recognize textual evidence to support claims provided by the teacher

Score 1.0

With help, the student can perform score 2.0 and 3.0 expectations.

Score 0.0

Even with help, the student cannot perform expectations.

Source: Adapted from Marzano et al., 2016, p. 52.

Figure E.3: Proficiency scale for claims, evidence, and reasoning.

Assessment

Source: Marzano et al., 2016, pp. 54–55.

Score 2.0—Please circle the letter of the correct response in items 1–5.

1. When we say that we have made an inference about a text, we mean that we have noticed something that is . . .

   a. directly stated

   b. indirectly hinted at

   c. explained in a footnote

   d. not present in the text at all

2. If you are writing an essay about a book and want to support your claim with textual evidence, the best thing to do would be . . .

   a. cite a direct quote

   b. paraphrase the text

   c. refer to a quote from an expert

   d. either a or b

3. Consider the following quote from *To Kill a Mockingbird* and then select the claim that it best supports: "Mockingbirds don't do one thing but make music for us to enjoy. They don't eat up people's gardens, don't nest in corncribs, they don't do one thing but sing their hearts out for us. That why it's a sin to kill a mockingbird" (Lee, 1960, p. 119).

   a. Children are often smarter than adults expect.

   b. Punishing innocent people is wrong.

   c. Some animals are pests.

   d. Always stand up for what you believe in.

4. Consider the following claim about *To Kill a Mockingbird* and select the quote that best supports it: In Maycomb, being masculine or manly means being physically able.

    a. "For some reason Dill had started crying and couldn't stop; quietly at first, then his sobs were heard by several people in the balcony" (Lee, 1960, p. 265).

    b. "Jem grabbed his left wrist and my right wrist, I grabbed my left wrist and Jem's right wrist, we crouched, and Dill sat on our saddle. We raised him and he caught the window sill" (Lee, 1960, p. 70).

    c. "Jem was scarlet. I pulled at his sleeve, and we were followed up the sidewalk by a philippic on our family's moral degeneration, the major premise of which was that half the Finches were in the asylum anyway, but if our mother were living we would not have come to such a state" (Lee, 1960, p. 136).

    d. "Our father didn't do anything. . . . Atticus did not drive a dump-truck for the county, he was not the sheriff, he did not farm, work in a garage, or do anything that could possibly arouse the admiration of anyone" (Lee, 1960, p. 118).

5. Consider the following claim about *To Kill a Mockingbird* and select the quote that best supports it: Women in the story are typically polite on the outside but cruel underneath.

    a. "I wondered at the world of women. . . . I must soon enter this world, where on its surface fragrant ladies rocked slowly, fanned gently, and drank cool water. But I was more at home in my father's world. People like Mr. Heck Tate did not trap you with innocent questions to make fun of you; even Jem was not highly critical unless you said something stupid" (Lee, 1960, pp. 312–313).

    b. "I felt the starched walls of a pink cotton penitentiary closing in on me, and for the second time in my life I thought of running away" (Lee, 1960, p. 182).

    c. "When we arrived at the Landing, Aunt Alexandra kissed Uncle Jack, Francis kissed Uncle Jack, Uncle Jimmy shook hands silently with Uncle Jack" (Lee, 1960, p. 107).

    d. "Miss Caroline was no more than twenty-one. She had bright auburn hair, pink cheeks, and wore crimson fingernail polish. She also wore high-heeled pumps and a red-and-white-striped dress. She looked and smelled like a peppermint drop" (Lee, 1960, p. 21).

Score 3.0—Please choose two of the three items to complete in this section of the assessment.

1. Examine the following three quotes from *To Kill a Mockingbird* and make a claim that is supported by all three. Then, explain how each quote supports your claim.

    "Miss Caroline seemed unaware that the ragged, denim-shirted and floursack-skirted first grade, most of whom had chopped cotton and fed hogs from the time they were able to walk, were immune to imaginative literature" (Lee, 1960, p. 22).

    "In Maycomb, if one went for a walk with no definite purpose in mind, it was correct to believe one's mind incapable of definite purpose" (Lee, 1960, p. 199).

    "[Atticus] did not do the things our schoolmates' fathers did: he never went hunting, he did not play poker or fish or drink or smoke. He sat in the livingroom and read" (Lee, 1960, p. 118).

2. Make a claim about the way most citizens of Maycomb treat children and the way Atticus treats children. Find at least two pieces of textual evidence to support your claim.

3. Make a claim about a theme or point that Harper Lee conveys through the story of Tom Robinson's arrest and trial. Use at least three pieces of textual evidence to support your claim.

Score 4.0

1. Make two opposing claims about a theme, character, relationship, or other situation in *To Kill a Mockingbird*. Support each claim with at least two pieces of textual evidence and then explain which claim is better supported.

Telling Time

Prioritized Standard: The student will tell and write time from analog and digital clocks to the nearest five minutes.

Scale

MEASUREMENT, DATA, STATISTICS, AND PROBABILITY		
Time		
Grade 2		
Score 4.0	In addition to score 3.0 performance, the student demonstrates in-depth inferences and applications that go beyond what was taught. The student will: • Solve real-world problems involving elapsed time • Write correct digital time from an analog clock and the reverse	
	Score 3.5 In addition to score 3.0 performance, partial success at score 4.0 content	
Score 3.0	The student will: • Tell and write time from analog clocks to the nearest five minutes (2.MD.7)	**Sample Activity:** What Time Is It? Materials: analog clock in the classroom Procedures: Periodically during the day, the student will tell or write the time, also indicating what he or she is doing at a particular time of the school day.
	Score 2.5 No major errors or omissions regarding score 2.0 content, and partial success at score 3.0 content	

Figure E.4: Proficiency scale for telling time, grade 2.

continued ⇨

Score 2.0	The student will recognize or recall specific vocabulary, such as: • *analog, clock, digital, minute, nearest, time, a.m., p.m.* The student will perform basic processes, such as: • Tell and write time from digital clocks to the nearest five minutes (2.MD.7) • Identify the hands on an analog clock • Count by fives to sixty • Tell time to the hour, half-hour, and quarter-hour • Write time using the correct format		**Sample Activities:** Beat the Timer Center Activity Materials: cards with different times to the five minutes; cards with digital clocks showing different times to the five minutes; egg timer Procedures: The student will match the times with the correct clock, trying to beat the egg timer.
	Score 1.5	Partial success at score 2.0 content, and major errors or omissions regarding score 3.0 content	
Score 1.0	With help, partial success at score 2.0 content and score 3.0 content		
	Score 0.5	With help, partial success at score 2.0 content but not at score 3.0 content	
Score 0.0	Even with help, no success		

Assessment

Level 2

1. Write the correct time on the blank under each clock.

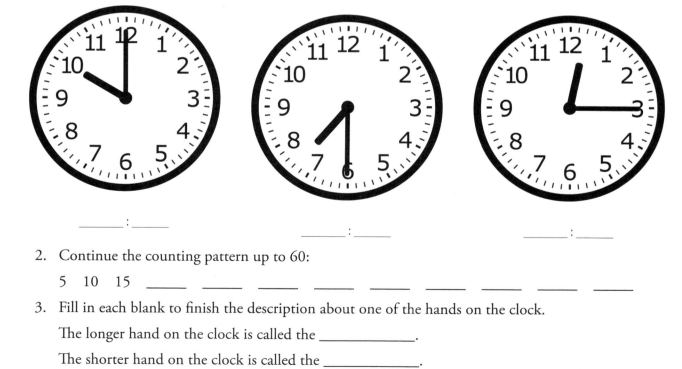

    _____ : _____   _____ : _____   _____ : _____

2. Continue the counting pattern up to 60:

    5   10   15   ____   ____   ____   ____   ____   ____   ____   ____   ____

3. Fill in each blank to finish the description about one of the hands on the clock.

    The longer hand on the clock is called the _____.

    The shorter hand on the clock is called the _____.

4. Read each time and write it in the box using the correct format.

Time	Correct Format
Four o'clock	
Forty-five minutes past eight	
Eleven-thirty	

5. Use the words from the box to answer the following questions.

Which word describes a clock that has a "face" and two "hands"? _____

Which word describes a time between midnight and noon? _____

Which word describes a time between noon and midnight? _____

Which word describes a clock that shows the time using numbers, not hands? _____

6. Write the time related to each digital clock to the nearest five minutes.

_____ : _____   _____ : _____   _____ : _____

Level 3

7. Write the correct time to the nearest five minutes on the blank below each clock.

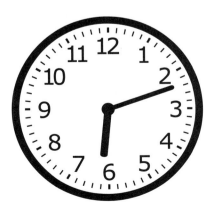      

_____ : _____   _____ : _____   _____ : _____

Level 4

8. Read the short word problem and answer the question.

   Robert began folding his clothes at 8:15 p.m. He was finished at 8:30 p.m. How long did he fold?

   _____ minutes

9. Solve this real-world problem involving elapsed time.

   The bus picks Jordan up at 7:45 a.m. He arrives at school at 8:50 a.m. How much time does Jordan spend riding on the bus to school each day?

   Jordan spends _____ minutes riding the bus to school each day.

The Hydrologic Cycle

Scale

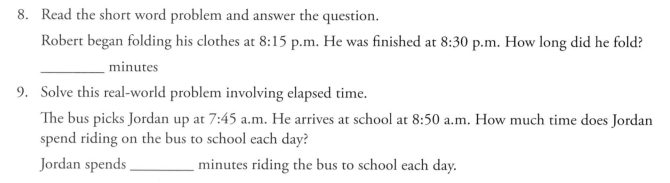

GRADE 6 SCIENCE The Hydrologic Cycle	
Score 4.0	I can explain how the hydrologic cycle is linked to pollution.
Score 3.0	I can develop a model to describe how water cycles through Earth's systems (including the importance of the sun's energy and the force of gravity).
Score 2.0	I can define each phase of the hydrologic cycle.
Score 1.0	With help, the student can demonstrate partial knowledge of the score 2.0 and 3.0 content.

Source: © 2019 by Columbus Public Schools. Used with permission.

Figure E.5: Proficiency scale for the hydrologic cycle, grade 6.

Assessment

Source: © 2019 by Columbus Public Schools. Used with permission.

Level 2

Answer the following questions to define each phase of the hydrologic cycle.

1. What is evaporation?
2. What is transpiration?
3. What are condensation and crystallization?
4. What is precipitation?
5. What is percolation?

Level 3

1. On a separate piece of paper, draw a model of the hydrologic cycle. Be sure to label all the parts of the cycle.

2. Use your model to write a paragraph to describe how water cycles through Earth's systems. Make sure you use academic vocabulary words within your description.

3. What role does the sun's energy play in the hydrologic cycle?

4. What role does the force of gravity play in the hydrologic cycle?

Level 4

1. How is the hydrologic cycle linked to pollution?

References

Anderson, L. W., & Krathwohl, D. R. (2001). *A taxonomy for learning, teaching, and assessing: A revision of Bloom's taxonomy of educational objectives* (Abridged ed.). Boston: Pearson.

Ainsworth, L. (2003). *Power standards: Identifying the standards that matter most.* Denver, CO: Advanced Learning Press.

Board of Regents of the University of Wisconsin System. (2018). *About | WIDA.* Accessed at https://wida.wisc.edu/about on July 2, 2019.

Georgia Department of Education. (2019). *Georgia standards of excellence.* Accessed at www.georgiastandards.org/Georgia-Standards/Pages/default.aspx on July 8, 2019.

Gottlieb, M., Cranley, M. E., & Oliver, A. R. (2007). *Understanding the WIDA English language proficiency standards.* Accessed at www.waunakee.k12.wi.us/newsfile18749_1.pdf on February 21, 2019.

Guskey, T. R. (2011). Five obstacles to grading reform. *Educational Leadership, 69*(3), 16–21.

Hattie, J. (2011). *Feedback in schools.* In R. Sutton, M. J. Horsey, & K. M. Douglas (Eds.), *Feedback: The communication of praise, criticism, and advice.* Accessed at www.visiblelearningplus.com/sites/default/files/Feedback%20article.pdf on June 17, 2019.

Heflebower, T., Hoegh, J. K., & Warrick, P. (2014). *A school leader's guide to standards-based grading.* Bloomington, IN: Marzano Resources.

Heflebower, T., Hoegh, J. K., Warrick, P., & Flygare, J. (2019). *A teacher's guide to standards-based learning.* Bloomington, IN: Marzano Resources.

Lee, H. (1960). *To kill a mockingbird.* New York: Grand Central.

Marzano, R. J. (2003). *What works in schools.* Alexandria, VA: Association for Supervision and Curriculum Development.

Marzano, R. J. (2006). *Classroom assessment and grading that work.* Alexandria, VA: Association for Supervision and Curriculum Development.

Marzano, R. J. (2009). *Designing and teaching learning goals and objectives.* Bloomington, IN: Marzano Resources.

Marzano, R. J. (2010). *Formative assessment and standards-based grading.* Bloomington, IN: Marzano Resources.

Marzano, R. J. (2017). *The new art and science of teaching.* Bloomington, IN: Solution Tree Press.

Marzano, R. J., & Haystead, M. W. (2008). *Making standards useful in the classroom.* Alexandria, VA: Association for Supervision and Curriculum Development.

Marzano, R. J., Heflebower, T., Hoegh, J. K., Warrick, P., & Grift, G. (with Hecker, L., & Wills, J.). (2016). *Collaborative teams that transform schools: The next step in PLCs.* Bloomington, IN: Marzano Resources.

Marzano, R. J. & Kendall, J. S. (1996). *A comprehensive guide to standards-based districts, schools, and classrooms.* Alexandria, VA: Association for Supervision and Curriculum Development.

Marzano, R. J., & Kendall, J. S. (1999). *Essential knowledge: The debate over what American students should know.* Denver, CO: McREL.

Marzano, R. J., & Kendall, J. S. (2007). *The new taxonomy of educational objectives* (2nd ed.). Alexandria, VA: Association for Supervision and Curriculum Development.

Marzano, R. J., Norford, J. S., & Ruyle, M. (2019). *The new art and science of classroom assessment.* Bloomington, IN: Solution Tree Press.

Marzano, R. J., Warrick, P. B., & Simms, J. A. (2014). *A handbook for high reliability schools: The next step in school reform.* Bloomington, IN: Marzano Resources.

Marzano, R. J., & Yanoski, D. C. (with Paynter, D. E.). (2016). *Proficiency scales for the new science standards: A framework for science instruction and assessment.* Bloomington, IN: Marzano Resources.

Marzano, R. J., Yanoski, D. C., Hoegh, J. K., & Simms, J. A. (2013). *Using Common Core standards to enhance classroom instruction and assessment.* Bloomington, IN: Marzano Resources.

McTighe, J. (2013). *Core learning: Assessing what matters most.* Provo, UT: School Improvement Network.

McTighe, J. (2017). *Designing authentic performance-based assessment tasks and rubrics* [Presentation handout]. Columbia, MD: McTighe and Associates.

Miller, K. (2018). *Bloom's Taxonomy and Webb's Depth of Knowledge* [Blog post]. Accessed at www.synergiseducation .com/blooms-taxonomy-and-webbs-depth-of-knowledge/ on February 21, 2019.

National Governors Association Center for Best Practices & Council of Chief State School Officers. (2010a). *Common Core State Standards for English language arts and literacy in history/social studies, science, and technical subjects.* Washington, DC: Authors. Accessed at www.corestandards.org/assets/CCSSI_ELA%20 Standards.pdf on July 8, 2019.

National Governors Association Center for Best Practices & Council of Chief State School Officers. (2010b). *Common Core State Standards for mathematics.* Washington, DC: Authors. Accessed at www.corestandards .org/assets/CCSSI_Math%20Standards.pdf on July 8, 2019.

Nebraska Department of Education. (2014). *Nebraska K–12 fine arts standards: Visual arts.* Accessed at http:// nde.ne.gov/FineArts/Standards/Final_FAS_Visual_Arts.pdf on July 1, 2019.

Simms, J. A. (2016). *The critical concepts.* Accessed at www.MarzanoResources.com/the-critical-concepts on February 21, 2019.

Smarter Balanced Assessment Consortium. (2012). *Smarter-Balanced argumentative writing rubric, grades 6–12.* Accessed at http://stevens.portangelesschools.org/common/pages/DisplayFile.aspx?itemId=8492059 on July 2, 2019.

Webb, N. L., et al. (2005). *Web alignment tool.* Accessed at https://static.pdesas.org/content/documents /M1-Slide_19_DOK_Wheel_Slide.pdf on June 25, 2019.

Wiggins, G. (2012). 7 keys to effective feedback. *Educational Leadership, 70*(1), 11–16.

Wyoming State Board of Education. (2014). *Career & vocational education content and performance standards.* Cheyenne: Wyoming Department of Education. Accessed at https://1ddlxtt2jowkvs672myo6z14-wpengine .netdna-ssl.com/wp-content/uploads/2018/12/2014-CVE-WyCPS-FINAL_11.28.18sd_FINAL.pdf on July 1, 2019.

Index

Professional Development Designed for Success

Empower your staff to tap into their full potential as educators. As an all-inclusive research-into-practice resource center, we are committed to helping your school or district become highly effective at preparing every student for his or her future.

Choose from our wide range of customized professional development opportunities for teachers, administrators, and district leaders. Each session offers hands-on support, personalized answers, and accessible strategies that can be put into practice immediately.

Bring Marzano Resources experts to your school for results-oriented training on:

- ▶ Assessment & Grading
- ▶ Curriculum
- ▶ Instruction
- ▶ School Leadership

- ▶ Teacher Effectiveness
- ▶ Student Engagement
- ▶ Vocabulary
- ▶ Competency-Based Education

LEARN MORE at MarzanoResources.com/PD